The Eighty-Five Martyrs

The Eighty-Five Martyrs

Roland Connelly

McCRIMMONS
Great Wakering Essex

First published in 1987 by McCrimmon Publishing Co Ltd
Great Wakering, Essex, England

ISBN 0 85597 405 2

Cover design by Paul Shuttleworth
Typeset by Barry Sarling, Rayleigh, Essex
Printed by Mayhew McCrimmon Printers Ltd
Great Wakering, Essex

Principal Sources of Information

Memoirs of the Missionary Priests, Bishop Richard Challoner, 1742.
First and Second Douai Diaries, ed. T.F. Knox, 1878.
The Troubles of our Catholic Forefathers, J. Morris SJ; 1872, 1875, 1877.
Lives of the English Martyrs, E.H. Burton and J.H. Pollen SJ, 1914.
Records of the English Province of the Society of Jesus, H. Foley SJ, 1877-1883.
The Seminary Priests, G. Anstruther OP, 1969-1977.
Publications of the Catholic Record Society.
Recusant History.
English and Welsh Priests, A. Bellenger OSB, 1984.

Foreword

In the lives of the eighty-five martyrs we find examples of courage, perseverance and integrity in the ordinary circumstances of daily life. The martyrs were not, by and large, rich and famous, nor would they have been known outside their immediate locality. Among the eighty-five we find a printer, 'a poor man that kept lodgings' and 'a simple serving man in an inn'. We also find those many priests who went abroad to study and returned knowing that they would be hunted and eventually executed. Most of them died young.

The stories of the martyrs are not simply historical records of past events. They are part of our heritage which lives on in the families descended from them and in those countless others whose ancestors helped priests to do their work in penal times. When we read these lives, we are reading about our own forebears and about people from families still in existence in our day.

Circumstances have changed. Happily we live now in a different age. We pray and work for Christian unity. Nothing, however, can take away from the fact that Catholics died with great courage for what they believed. We are immensely proud of our martyrs.

Fr. Roland Connelly has once again put us in his debt by providing us with these eighty-five brief biographies.

Cardinal Archbishop of Westminster

The Mass House, Egton Bridge, Yorkshire (since rebuilt); traditionally associated with Nicholas Postgate (picture by B. McCoy)

Introduction

The attempt is made in these pages to present brief, factual accounts of the lives and deaths of the eighty-five English and Welsh Martyrs who suffered for their Catholic Faith between the years 1584 and 1679 and who are to be beatified by Pope John Paul II in Rome on 22 November, 1987.

If more space has been allocated to some martyrs and less to others, this should not be seen as indicative of their relative importance and should certainly not be attributed to the personal preference of the writer. The reason lies solely in the availability of information. In the sixteenth and seventeenth centuries the keeping of records was not a high priority and Catholics in particular were very slow to commit themselves to writing lest they provided evidence to incriminate themselves or their friends. In the ensuing centuries, the passage of time has taken its toll, many documents have been lost or mislaid and some are known to have been destroyed. In such circumstances, it is inevitable today that much more is known about some martyrs than about others, and that, in any narrative, disconcerting gaps will frequently mar the continuity of information.

Catholics understand very well that a martyr is a martyr because he died a holy death. Most martyrs did in fact also lead holy lives but it is the manner of their death which is most important, and the martyr's contemporaries concerned themselves more about the details of his death than those of his life. There is, accordingly, convincing proof that each of these eighty-five martyrs died for his Faith, and indeed at times such an abundance of harrowing detail that a process of selection is required. Modern Catholics may be disappointed that so little is known about the lives of some of the martyrs and no doubt more details will emerge as historical research continues, but for the moment the character of the living man must often be deduced from the way he died.

It is sad that not all those heroic men and women who died for their Faith during the English persecution have received proper recognition. Many have been forgotten; many simply disappeared into prison to die a lonely death unknown to their friends and neighbours; many died on the scaffold, but the validity of their martyrdom cannot be proved. Such martyrs are known to God alone and receive no individual veneration from the Church on earth.

The Church does not make martyrs but the Church is constantly aware that many of her children have preferred death to infidelity and she seeks by every means possible to identify her martyrs and honour them. To do this prudently demands a very detailed investigation by specially appointed theologians and historians. This is far from being a superficial examination; it usually lasts for many years and sometimes several centuries as these experts seek definitive answers to three vital questions:

1) Did this person die because of his loyalty to God and His Church?
2) Did he freely accept this death?
3) Did contemporary Catholics accept him as a true martyr for the Faith?

The Process of Canonisation

In the ordinary course of events, a martyr is first recognised and unofficially honoured by those who know him best: his friends, his neighbours, and witnesses to his execution. By word and letter the information is passed on to other people who accept the facts and share in the devotion. When the local Bishop is satisfied that a reputable cult has developed he sets up his own diocesan commission of enquiry and the results are reported to the Roman authorities for further consideration.

Under the old legislation prior to 1913, as soon as the candidate was accepted for consideration by the Papal enquiry, he was entitled to be called Venerable. Later, if the matter developed satisfactorily, a stage would be reached when the Pope declared the martyr to be Blessed. This is the preliminary stage to canonisation as a Saint and means, in effect that the martyr may be honoured in public devotions and the liturgy as if he were a saint, but that this veneration is restricted to certain groups of people or specified localities. Only after much more searching enquiry is the Blessed Martyr proclaimed to be a Saint of the Universal Church.

During the sixteenth and seventeenth centuries in England, many Catholics died as a result of religious persecution. Some of them were immediately recognised as martyrs. At times, even as the condemned man approached the scaffold he was saluted as a martyr by his brothers and sisters in the Faith. Catholics were secretly present at trials and executions because they had no doubt that they were witnessing true martyrdom. Frequently attempts were made after the execution to collect souvenirs of the dead man and relics of his person. These were carefully preserved as objects of religious devotion. A popular cult of veneration grew up in a spontaneous manner and information was proudly sent to other Catholic communities at home and overseas.

The English Martyrs

Devotion to the English Martyrs was established in the city of Rome by 1583 when frescoes depicting sixty-three Martyrs were painted and then publicly exhibited in the Venerable English College as a confident sign of an existing veneration. In 1626, Pope Urban VIII sought further information from Bishop Richard Smith, the newly appointed Vicar Apostolic in England, and the Bishop attested to his own belief in the validity of many martyrdoms and produced for the Pope his own list of known martyrs in his Chalcedon Catalogue.

A papal commission of enquiry was set up in 1643 at the direct request of the English Benedictine monks, and as there were no diocesan bishops in England at that time, the Archbishop of Cambrai in France was appointed 'to collect and examine the evidence for the cause, fact and constancy of martyrdom of all those who were known to have suffered for the Faith up to that time'. Efforts were made to collect evidence in England but, with persecution raging, it was a hazardous undertaking and was soon discontinued.

It was not until 1850, when the English Hierarchy of Bishops was restored, that work on the recognition of the martyrs could recommence. In the calmer religious atmosphere of Victorian England scholarly investigations could be pursued and results obtained.

In 1886 Pope Leo XIII pronounced on the merits of 361 English Martyrs and accepted 318 of them as true martyrs for the Faith. 255 of these martyrs were declared to be Venerable and another 63 to be Blessed.

In 1935 two of the Blessed Martyrs, Thomas More and John Fisher, were canonised as Saints and in 1970 the Forty Martyrs were also canonised.

Of the 255 Venerable Martyrs named in the 1886 declaration, 136 were beatified in 1929, but at that time it was decided that more information was needed about the remaining 119 'in order that their martyrdom might be more clearly manifested'. Subsequently, 85 of these 'dilati' or delayed martyrs have been cleared for beatification and these are the martyrs described in this book.

All these eighty-five martyrs figure prominently in the various Catalogues of Martyrs compiled by their contemporaries from 1586 until 1681. That they truly died for their Faith is demonstrated from the very nature of the laws under which they suffered. Seventy-six of them were executed because they contravened the Elizabethan Statute of 1585 'against Jesuits, seminary priests and such other like disobedient persons', which made it high treason for any Englishman ordained overseas as a Catholic priest to come into or remain in England and a capital felony for anyone to harbour or assist him. Two others were executed under the old treason act of 1352 and six under the act of 1581, which made it high treason to be reconciled or to reconcile someone else to the Catholic Church.

Honouring the Martyrs Today

As Catholics honour their martyrs today they do so in the religious atmosphere of the modern world where ecumenical endeavours among the various Christian churches play such an important role. Devotion to the martyrs should not be seen as an attempt to re-open the old wounds of bitterness and division which formerly existed between the different denominations. Martyrs are religious heroes who can be admired even when the cause for which they suffered may not be accepted.

If some Catholics are still uneasy and embarrassed about the ecumenical implications of devotion to the martyrs then they should listen carefully to the voices from other churches and the repeated assurances of sympathetic understanding from those who do not share the Catholic Faith. The British Council of Churches declared in 1969 that 'the different Christian denominations all acknowledge the martyr tradition as one in which all have shared and from which all may draw strength even across denominational boundaries', and early in 1987 the Archbishop of Canterbury, Dr Robert Runcie, courteously expressed the hope that the beatification of these eighty-five Martyrs would prompt all Christians 'to pursue the path of reconciliation and reunion with greater understanding and effectiveness'.

And is it not true, as Pope Paul VI pointed out so clearly at the canonisation ceremonies for the Forty Martyrs in 1970, that the real witness of the English Catholic Martyrs is to the unity of God's Church? It was in an effort to preserve that unity that they so willingly gave their lives.

1. William Carter layman

Born in London about 1550
Hanged, drawn and quartered at Tyburn, London on 11 January, 1584, aged about 34

WILLIAM CARTER was a printer and an active Catholic in defiance of Queen Elizabeth's laws. As private secretary to the prominent Catholic writer, Dr Nicholas Harpsfield (in Catholic days the Archdeacon of Canterbury), he had ready access to much Catholic information and was able to print and publish many Catholic books which were forbidden by the Government.

The existence of the secret printing press was however known to the civil authorities, and the identity of the printer suspected. William Carter was in prison for his Faith in 1578 and again in 1579, and the Protestant Bishop of London, John Aylmer, reported to Lord Burghley that a printing press and 'naughty papistical books' had been found in the house of 'one Carter, a very lewd fellow, who hath been divers times before in prison for printing of lewd pamphlets'.

In July 1582 William Carter was arrested again and subjected to torture in the Tower of London but even in circumstances of excruciating pain he refused to give any information about his accomplices.

English law at that time did not lend itself easily to securing a sentence of death for religious offences, and so William Carter was charged under the ancient Treason Act of 1352, that by printing his Catholic books he was inciting the people of England to murder their Queen. At his trial, much emphasis was given to Dr Gregory Martin's *Treatise of Schisme*, which Carter had printed and which included a passage referring to the episode in the Book of Judith where the valiant Judith cuts off the head of the King Holofernes

(Judith 13:1-12). The passage, quite innocuous in itself, was misconstrued as an encouragement to English women to follow the example of Judith and cut off the head of their Monarch.

In court, Sir John Popham, the Attorney General, claimed that the *Treatise of Schisme* was 'written by a traitor', (Gregory Martin), 'approved by a traitor,' (Cardinal William Allen) and 'addressed to traitors' (the English Catholics). Cardinal Allen replied a few months later that Carter 'was a poor innocent artisan, made away only for printing a Catholic book in which no word was found against the State, the quarrel only most unjustly being made upon a certain clause which by no likely honest construction could appertain to the Queen's person'.

On the strength of this textual misinterpretation, William Carter was found guilty of treachery and was duly executed.

2. *George Haydock* seminary priest

Born at Cottam Hall, near Preston, Lancashire about 1557
Hanged, drawn and quartered at Tyburn, London on 12 February, 1584, aged about 27

GEORGE HAYDOCK came from a staunchly Catholic family and was about sixteen years of age when he entered the English College, Douai. Later he proceeded to the Venerable English College at Rome but ill-health demanded his return to more suitable northern climates and he was ordained priest at Soissons on 21 December 1581.

Father Haydock's journey to the dangers of London began on 16 January 1582 and he found lodgings near St Paul's Churchyard. Within one month he had the misfortune to be betrayed by a false friend. By his own testimony, before he could celebrate his first Mass in England he was in prison.

For the next fifteen months he endured solitary confinement in the Tower. At this time, his only visitors were Protestant scholars and clergymen who tried to break his spirit by frequent theological disputations. He became so exasperated that he expressed his convictions by writing over the door of his cell, 'Gregory XIII is Head of the English and of the Universal Church, to whom both Queen Elizabeth and all the rest of the world must be subject if they wish to be saved'.

Father Haydock was one of the fourteen priests brought before the Queen's Bench at Westminster on 5 February 1584, and with them he was accused of conspiring at Rheims to raise a rebellion in England to depose and kill the Queen. The fact that he was not in Rheims at the time stated for the conspiracy was not allowed to diminish the strength of the evidence and for this fictitious plot he was condemned to death.

On 12 February 1584, in company with four other condemned priests, Thomas Hemerford, James Fenn, John Nutter and John Munden, Father Haydock was dragged through the city streets on a rough hurdle from the Tower to Tyburn. On the scaffold, he prayed calmly for his own salvation and for his country and then bravely stepped forward as the first of the five victims to be hanged, drawn and quartered.

3. *Hugh Taylor* seminary priest

Born at Durham about 1560
Hanged, drawn and quartered at York on 26 November, 1585, aged about 25

In 1585 QUEEN ELIZABETH passed a new and dreadful law against her Catholic subjects. It was called 'An Act against Jesuits, seminary priests and such other like disobedient persons' and was intended to widen the scope of the existing treachery laws so that it became high treason for any Englishman ordained abroad as a Catholic priest after 24 June 1559 to come into or to remain in England. Henceforward, it was not necessary to prove that a Catholic priest was plotting against his Queen; he became a traitor by merely setting foot in his own country.

Father Hugh Taylor was the first Catholic priest to be charged under the provisions of this new Act. Admitted to the English

College, then at Rheims, on 7 May 1582, and ordained after two years study on 13 June 1584, Father Taylor had begun his missionary apostolate in Yorkshire and Durham about the month of March, 1585. Within another eight months he was on trial for his life.

He was captured by Lord Evers 'when he searched a Catholic man's house' somewhere in Yorkshire and was brought before the Council of the North in York. Father John Mush who was living in York at that time has stated 'They alleged no other matter against him but that he was a seminary priest...' For this he was condemned to death.

An anonymous paper of 1586 in Father Christopher Grene's Collection E describes the priest's final hours: 'Taylor, having been condemned to death in company with a layman on Thursday, was able to celebrate Mass and recite his Office on the Friday. Then he said, "How happy I should be if on this day on which Christ died for me, I might encounter death for him". Scarcely had he said this, when the officer unexpectedly came to lead him off to execution, and leaving the layman for Saturday, (the customary day for executions) put him immediately to death'.

4. *Marmaduke Bowes* layman

Born at Angram Grange, near Osmotherley, Yorkshire; date unknown
Hanged at York on 27 November, 1585

In THE CHALCEDON RETURNS of 1620 Bishop Richard Smith, Vicar Apostolic of England, lends his authority to Mr Leonard Brackenbury's report that Bowes was executed merely for giving a cup of beer at his door to a priest. Another contemporary, Mr John Ingleby, relates how Mr Bowes, hearing that his friend, Father Hugh Taylor, was on trial for his life at York, immediately took horse for the city; and, without pausing even to remove his boots and spurs, burst into the court-room where he defended the priest with such vehemence that he incriminated himself, and was executed with such speed that he was still wearing his boots and spurs on the scaffold.

Both stories are typical of Mr Bowes. 'He was wonderfully beloved and well spoken of among his neighbours', wrote Father John Mush who knew him personally, and then added, 'He thought it a desperate point of impiety to shut up his hospitality from priests...and to these men, I say, he opened his doors bountifully'.

And yet Marmaduke Bowes in his life was not fully a Catholic. In a country where there were no bishops and very few priests, laymen had to make their own theological decisions and many conformed outwardly to the Anglican Church while remaining Catholic in their hearts. Marmaduke Bowes lived a life of pretence as one of these Church Papists. His wife and children remained fully Catholic though, and sadly it was the Catholic teacher he employed for his children who betrayed him to the authorities for welcoming priests to his house.

The Council of the North found Marmaduke Bowes guilty of contravening the new statute 'against Jesuits, seminary priests and such other like disobedient persons', which contained a provision against any layperson 'harbouring' or helping a priest. He was the first layman to be condemned to death under this Statute.

Father John Mush reports his full reconciliation in prison, probably by Father Hugh Taylor. As a layman he escaped the horrible death of being hanged, drawn and quartered; he was simply hanged.

5. Nicholas Woodfen seminary priest

Born at Leominster, Herefordshire about 1550
Hanged, drawn and quartered at Tyburn, London on 21 January, 1586, aged about 36

According to his old schoolfellow, Father Richard Davies, Nicholas Woodfen was originally called Nicholas Wheler and 'held for one of the best scholars in the school'. (Westminster

Archives A III, p.239). Later, Woodfen worked as an assistant to St Swithun Wells in the school at Monkton Farleigh in Wiltshire and probably spent some time in London before presenting himself at the English College in Rheims on 27 December 1579. He was ordained priest by the Bishop of Châlons-sur-Marne on 25 March 1581, and set out for the English Missions on 30 June.

The newly-ordained priest attempted to settle in London but experienced great poverty. Father Richard Davies describes how he met him secretly in an inn where he 'declared unto me, (the tears standing in his eyes) that he had neither money to buy him meat nor scarce any clothes upon his back. I pitied his case, comforted him and gave him such money as I had then present.'

With the help of Father Davies, Father Woodfen obtained lodgings in Fleet Street, near the conduit and not far from the Inns of Court. From this base he devoted himself to a special apostolate among the lawyers and students who frequented the area. The priest mingled with them freely, wearing a gown as one of them, and so successful was his work for the Church that a Government spy, Thomas Dodwell, claimed he was one of 'the most traitorous papists of that seminary of Satan' and insisted that he be 'apprehended with as much speed as maybe'. (Foley: *Records SJ* VI, pp.722-6)

The pressure was on Father Woodfen. Father Davies states that Norris, the pursuivant 'ferreted him out' of Fleet Street. He took refuge with Father Davies at Hoxton and both priests had a very narrow escape when the house was searched and they were forced to take safety in the priest's hiding hole.

No information is available as to when and how Father Nicholas Woodfen was captured by the authorities, but he was condemned for his priesthood at the Newgate Sessions at the Old Bailey on 19 January 1586, and suffered death in company with Blessed Edward Stransham at Tyburn two days later.

6. *Richard Sergeant* seminary priest

Born in Gloucestershire about 1550 (?)
Hanged, drawn and quartered at Tyburn, London on 20 April, 1586, aged about 36 (?)

RICHARD SERGEANT'S place of birth is given vaguely as Gloucestershire; his date of birth is a tentative calculation. That he graduated from Oxford University in February 1571 is established from Boase and Clark (I, p.281) but for the next ten years his life is unrecorded.

The Douai Diary announced the arrival of Richard Sergeant at the English College in Rheims on 25 July 1581, and from the same source it is known that he was ordained priest at Laon on 7 April 1583, and departed for the English Mission on 10 September of the same year.

Father Richard Sergeant preserved his freedom for less than three years. It is presumed that he worked in the London area. Dr Anthony Champney (c. 1618) made a general reference to 'his fruitful labours on the English Mission' (Westminster Archives F 1, p.833), and in his Memoirs of Missionary Priests (1741) Bishop Richard Challoner described Father Sergeant as a man of learning, who had laboured for some time in gaining souls to Christ.

Father Sergeant's next appearance in the records is for his trial and execution. In company with Father William Thomson he was charged at the Newgate Sessions at the Old Bailey on 18 April 1586, and both were condemned and executed for their priesthood.

7. *William Thomson* seminary priest

Born at Blackburn, Lancashire about 1560
Hanged, drawn and quartered at Tyburn, London on 20 April, 1586, aged about 26

THE DOUAI DIARY records that William Thomson entered the English College at Rheims on 28 May 1583, and that having completed his studies in less than twelve months, he was ordained priest on 31 March 1584.

Father Thomson seems to have devoted himself to the London

Mission and in the writings of that time there are several tantalising glimpses of his activities. According to Father John Gerard SJ (*Autobiography of an Elizabethan*, p.82) Father Thomson first took up residence at the house of William Heigham (the brother of St Anne Line), who protected him. In March 1585 a spy reported to the Secretary of State, Sir Francis Walsingham, that 'one Thomson' was frequenting the house in Ely Place of another well known Catholic, Sir John Arundell, but it is not certain that this is William Thomson the priest. Another spy reported on 26 May 1585, that 'Blackburn' (Father Thomson's alias) was one of eleven priests 'now lodged in common inns about London'. (*Troubles of our Catholic Forefathers*, II, p.158)

In the winter of 1585-6 a series of exorcisms was carried out, chiefly at Denham in Buckinghamshire, and again a Thomson is mentioned as one of those present, but positive identification poses problems.

There are two accounts of Father William Thomson's arrest. One is based on the Prison List reprinted in Vol. II, p.249 of the Catholic Record Society's publications. This shows that on 14 June 1586, William Heigham and Roger Line (St Anne Line's brother and her husband), were both prisoners for their Faith and adds the information that 'they were taken at Bishopsgate Without at Mass with Blackburn alias Thomson that was hanged'. It is not clear whether Father Thomson was arrested on this occasion or whether he managed to escape. Another account suggests a later arrest after another Mass celebrated by Father Thomson at Robert Bellamy's house at Harrow on the Hill.

Whatever the details of his arrest may be, William Thomson was in custody with Father Richard Sergeant and they appeared together before the Newgate Sessions at the Old Bailey on 18 April 1586, to receive their sentence of death.

8. *Francis Ingleby* seminary priest

Born at Ripley Castle, West Yorkshire about 1550
Hanged, drawn and quartered at York on 3 June, 1586, aged about 36

THE INGLEBY FAMILY was one of the most powerful gentry families in Yorkshire and among the strongest supporters of Catholicism in the county. Francis, the fourth son, was educated at Brasenose College, Oxford, and then went on to study law at the Inner Temple in London. All these studies he abandoned in 1582 to cross the seas to Rheims where he entered the English College on 18 August and was ordained priest on 17 December 1583.

On his return to England, Father Ingleby worked for two years as a missionary priest in the city of York and assisted Father Richard Holtby SJ and Father John Mush in their reorganisation of the mission. He was well known to St Margaret Clitherow and was one of the priests that the Flemish boy accused her of harbouring in her 'hide' in the Shambles. When St Margaret was arrested on 10 March 1586, the whole mission was thrown into disarray and the priests dispersed. Father Ingleby was unfortunate: a layman accompanied him out of the city towards safety, but on taking his leave showed too much respect for the shabbily dressed priest and the suspicions of bystanders were aroused. Father Ingleby was arrested and taken before the Council of the North.

The trial took place on 2 June 1586, and after some very unsatisfactory, quasi-legal proceedings, Father Ingleby was condemned to death as a traitor. As he was taken back to York Castle after the trial to await his execution, the loyal Catholics of York made a great demonstration and changed his pathetic procession into a march of triumph. They leaned out of their windows, cheered him and shouted for his blessing.

Next day, the authorities made sure to control the crowd and as Father Ingleby was dragged on his hurdle through the cobbled streets to his death at the Knavesmire, the Catholics could only watched from a distance in sympathetic silence and proud prayer as another martyr prepared to receive his crown.

9. John Fingley seminary priest

Born at Barmby in the Marsh, near Howden, North Humberside, in 1553
Hanged, drawn and quartered at York on 8 August, 1586, aged 33

JOHN FINGLEY came from a poor family of farmers in the rich agricultural district of Howdenshire where the powerful family of the Babthorpes exercised a strong Catholic influence. He was a young man of great ability and in 1573 secured admission to Gonville and Caius College in the University of Cambridge on the understanding that he would be expected to work as one of the College servants in return for free lodging and tuition.

A major dispute however broke out in the College in 1574 when the Master, Dr Thomas Legge, a Catholic, appointed Fingley to the prestigious office of Butler. The Fellows complained that Fingley was only appointed because he was a Catholic and strong anti-Catholic feelings were manifested. In the *Caian*, (vol. 1 p.169 and vol. 5 p.152), J. Venn relates that Fingley was described as 'an arrant papist' and 'a great perverter of youth' and he adds the information that Fingley was reputed to be a priest and had said Mass in 'the Master's greater chamber over the parlour'.

In fact John Fingley was not yet a priest. He left the University without a degree and was admitted to the English College at Rheims on 13 February 1580. He was ordained priest on 25 March 1581 and returned to the English Mission, where he preserved his freedom for four years.

Towards the end of June 1585 Father Fingley was captured in Yorkshire and taken to a squalid cell in Peter Prison, York. Here he had a strange encounter with one of the most valiant Catholic women of those difficult times, Miss Frances Webster, who was enduring solitary confinement in the cell immediately above that occupied by the priest. She managed to open a grate 'to let in some light unto him in the darkness', gave him a gown to keep him warm and encouraged him with her words of faith. Very shortly after this encounter Miss Webster died, still a prisoner for her faith. This was on 29 June.

Father John Fingley was brought to trial at York, probably at the Summer Assizes of 1586, and condemned to death for his priesthood. His mother is said to have watched her son's execution.

10. *John Sandys* seminary priest

Born in Lancashire about 1550-1555
Hanged, drawn and quartered at Gloucester on 11 August, 1586, aged between 31-36

JOHN SANDYS graduated from Oriel College, Oxford, in 1573 and became tutor to the children of Admiral Sir William Winter at Lydney in Gloucestershire. At first he was not a Catholic but was later reconciled to Rome. He was admitted to the English College at Rheims on 4 June 1583, and ordained priest in Rheims Cathedral on 31 March 1584.

In company with Father John Owen and Father John Lister, Father Sandys sailed from Dieppe for England and landed close to Rye in Sussex. From there he made his way alone back to Gloucestershire and the friends he had made while working at Lydney. For almost two years he was undisturbed in this apostolate and as Bishop Richard Challoner says, 'he diligently applied himself to his missionary functions'.

The circumstances of the arrest of Father Sandys in the summer of 1586 are described in a document of c. 1587 in the Archives of the English College, Rome. (*Scritture*, 21.2.2.) The priest was visiting or staying with his friend the Anglican Dean of Lydney, who may or may not have known that he was entertaining a priest. Certainly some of the Dean's enemies knew the true identity of the Dean's guest and sought to hurt him by arranging for the priest to be apprehended while in his company. They gave no thought to the fate of the priest; all they wanted to do was hurt the Dean.

The plan misfired. Father Sandys was arrested in the Dean's company, but the Dean insisted that he had no knowledge that Father Sandys was a priest and was cleared. The priest was taken to prison. The perpetrators of the trick visited him in his cell to apologise and assure him that they had meant him no harm but they could do nothing to impede the due process of law.

Father Sandys was tried in Gloucester at the Summer Assizes of 1586 and sentenced to death for his priesthood. On the morning of his execution he was allowed to celebrate Mass and afterwards with great courage he exhorted his small congregation to persevere in the Faith.

The manner of his death was an exhibition of extreme cruelty. An experienced and clumsy executioner produced a horrifying spectacle which upset even those bystanders who were accustomed to the barbarities of rope and knife. Many non-Catholics shouted their protest and praised the bravery of the priest, and afterwards many Protestant clergymen condemned the whole affair in their sermons.

11. Robert Bickerdike layman

Born at Low Hall, Farnham, near Knaresborough, Yorkshire; date unknown
Hanged, drawn and quartered at York, towards the end of August 1586

ROBERT BICKERDIKE was a young and enthusiastic Catholic who did not hesitate to proclaim his religion openly even to the point of indiscretion. In the city of York he was well known as a Catholic, and was first arrested in 1585 when he was seen in the company of a Catholic priest, Father (now Saint) John Boste. A document of 1585 (attributed to Father John Mush) in Grene's Collection E maintains that Bickerdike was arrested because he and Father Boste were 'seen drinking together and the heretics surmised that this young man paid for the pot of ale, which they thought was matter sufficient to hang him'.

When he came to trial, Bickerdike also faced a charge of speaking treasonable words in so much as he had said to a fellow apprentice, 'The sap is with the Catholics in the root of the tree, but yet may perhaps ascend upwards towards Michaelmas and then he would use no such railing words' (*ibid.*); these words were taken to be a reference to the projected Spanish invasion and consequently a threat to the Queen. The members of the jury were not impressed by the evidence produced and the prisoner was acquitted; the judge, however, with a fine disregard for English law, ordered Bickerdike to be returned to prison to be tried again on the same charges at the next Assizes.

The second trial took place at the Summer Assizes in the Guildhall before the Judges of the Bench, Clench and Rodes, who questioned Bickerdike about the previous charges. The young man replied that he had been cleared of those charges a year before. So the judges tried to trick him with the famous 'bloody' question. What would he do if England were invaded by the Pope? Would he fight for the Pope or his Queen? Bickerdike replied with great wisdom that 'he could not tell in time before, what he would do in time to come. But, quoth he, I will do as it shall please God to put me in mind' (*ibid.*). This reply so angered the judges that they insulted him and called him traitor, and their obvious malice shocked the members of the jury so much that once more the prisoner was declared not guilty.

The farce continued. The judges assured Robert Bickerdike that 'he would not escape them,' and ordered him back to prison to await another trial.

When the third trial began, the judge had found a new jury and informed them that 'This traitor had too favourable and too scrupulous a jury in town, but I trust you will look otherwise to him, being the Queen's enemy and a notorious traitor' (*ibid*). The jury listened and obeyed; Robert Bickerdike was found guilty under the Statute of 1581 which had made it a capital offence to attempt to make converts to Rome. He was sentenced to be hanged, drawn and quartered.

12. *John Lowe* seminary priest

Born in London in 1553
Hanged, drawn and quartered at Tyburn, London on 8 October, 1586, aged 33

JOHN LOWE was the son of Simon and Margaret Lowe of London Bridge and entered the English College at Douai about the year 1575. His special abilities were recognised by the President of the College, Dr William Allen, who sent him to the Venerable English College in Rome, where he arrived on 19 November 1581. He was ordained priest in September 1582 and for some time contemplated a Jesuit vocation before returning to England as a seminary priest in late December, 1583.

Father Lowe worked on the English Mission for more than two years and seems to have settled in the London area. His presence was reported to Sir Francis Walsingham, Secretary of State, by one of the Government spies in March, 1585. At this time he was said to be frequenting the house of Mr Tremayne at Clerkenwell, then on the outskirts of the city.

The following year on 11 May, Father Lowe was arrested and committed to prison in the Clink, where a few months later he met Anthony Tyrrell, a Catholic priest who had turned spy for the Government. After some very careful consideration Father Lowe accepted Tyrell for what he pretended to be: a sincere Catholic and a priest in good standing. The result was that Tyrrell was able to collect sufficient evidence to denounce the priest to Justice Richard Young.

In company with Father John Adams and Father Robert Dibdale, Father John Lowe appeared before the Newgate Sessions at the Old Bailey, probably on 7 October 1586. All three were condemned to death and executed for being priests.

13. John Adams seminary priest

Born at Winterbourne St Martin in Dorsetshire about 1543
Hanged, drawn and quartered at Tyburn, London on 8 October, 1586, aged about 43

JOHN ADAMS was a member of the Established Church and Vicar of his native parish when he was converted to Catholicism. He presented himself at the English College at Rheims on 7 December 1579, and was ordained priest twelve months later.

With high aspirations, Father Adams set out for the English Mission on 29 March 1581, but was arrested on landing at Rye in Sussex and sent to London as a prisoner. In due time he affected his escape and by the end of June was safely back in Rheims, bringing with him, quite audaciously, some young students for the College.

Father Adams did not linger in Rheims. Within a few days of his return he set out again for England and for about six months was able to retain his freedom and work as a priest in Hampshire. On 7 March 1584, he was again arrested and spent the next eighteen months in the Marshalsea prison in London, before being banished from the Kingdom. Once more he returned to the safety of Rheims but again stayed only a few days while making his preparations for his third and last attempt on England.

Father Adams left Rheims in mid-November 1585 and made his way to Winchester, where he was arrested on 19 December and committed to the Clink prison in London. Here he was betrayed by Anthony Tyrrell just as Father John Lowe had been, and, together with Father Robert Dibdale, they shared the same scaffold.

14. Robert Dibdale seminary priest

Born at Shottery, Stratford-upon-Avon, Warwickshire, about 1558
Hanged, drawn and quartered at Tyburn, London, on 8 October, 1586, aged about 28

ROBERT DIBDALE was reported to be in Louvain in 1576 and arrived at the English College at Rheims from Rome on 29 December 1579, but it is not at all clear that these journeyings had any connection with preparation for the priesthood.

On 22 June 1580, Dibdale accompanied Father Edward Pole from Rheims to England but the priest was arrested on landing at Dover and within a short time both Pole and Dibdale were in prison at the Gatehouse at Westminster. Middlesex County Records show that during this time in prison, Robert Dibdale was charged and punished four times at the Middlesex Sessions for failing to attend the services of the Established Church.

Having served more than two years in prison he was released in September 1582, and six months later, on 14 March 1583, he returned to the English College at Rheims. This time it is certain that he was preparing for the priesthood, and he was ordained at Rheims on 31 March 1584.

Father Dibdale worked as a priest in the London area and was involved in 1585-6 in a controversial series of exorcisms performed by several priests under the leadership of Father William Weston SJ. These rituals took place at Edmund Peckham's house at Denham in Buckinghamshire and at other places closer to London and they excited much attention from Catholics and non-Catholics alike.

Later, on 24 July 1586, Father Dibdale had the misfortune to be recognised as a priest while walking along Tothill Street in Westminster. He was taken by the pursuivants, Newall and Worsley, to the Counter prison in Wood Street. From there he was removed to Newgate prison to be charged with Father John Lowe and Father John Adams at the Newgate Sessions, and with them he was found guilty and executed for his priesthood.

15. Alexander Crowe seminary priest

Born at Howden, Yorkshire in 1550
Hanged, drawn and quartered at York on 30 November, 1586, aged 36

ALEXANDER CROWE was a cobbler, possibly in Howden, certainly in York. He crossed the seas to the English College at Rheims in 1581. His purpose was to help. Perhaps he already had the priesthood in mind but his first tasks were menial. Dr Humphrey Ely in 1603 described him as 'first a cobbler, then a porter, after that under-cook in the seminary and at last by his extreme diligence got as much learning as was sufficient for a priest'.

Alexander Crowe was ordained priest on 17 December 1583, and by the beginning of March, 1584, was working on the East Yorkshire mission. Father Richard Holtby SJ, his ecclesiastical superior in York, wrote in 1590 that he was 'a man burning with zeal for souls, who therefore never refused any labour by which he could win them' and he added later that he usually travelled round his huge district on foot. For eighteen months Father Crowe served the Catholics of his own home area but towards the end of 1586 he was captured when he was summoned at night to South Duffield to minister to a Catholic woman, Cecily Garnett, who wished to follow the Catholic custom of her day and have her baby baptised as soon as it was born.

In Grene's Collection E there are two papers about Father Crowe's sufferings in prison in York. One attributed to Father John Mush describes how the priest was put in double fetters among the criminals; the other attributed to Father Richard Holtby SJ adds that conditions in prison were so bad that Father Crowe picked up a fever which stayed with him until death.

Both accounts converge to give a vivid picture of the trial. At the height of his fever Father Crowe was dragged from his bed and brought into court. He carried a small wooden cross which he had made himself but the gaolers snatched it from him and smashed it. He had shaved the crown of his head in a priestly tonsure so that instead of hiding his priesthood he was proudly flaunting it. He had no hope of an acquittal; he welcomed the sentence of death and praised God for His goodness.

In prison, the night before his execution, Father Crowe had a most extraordinary mystical experience, in which he was first troubled by the Devil and then strengthened by Our Lady and St John the Evangelist. This vision was well-authenticated by an eye-witness, and powerful evidence collected by Father Joseph Creswell SJ, Rector of the English College, Rome 1589-92, is included (pp.125-131) in the book *Historia Particular de la Persecucion de Inglaterra* written in 1599 by Diego de Yepes, Bishop of Tarragona in Spain.

16. Thomas Pilcher

seminary priest

Born at Battle in Sussex in 1557
Hanged, drawn and quartered at Dorchester on 21 March, 1587, aged 30

THOMAS PILCHER graduated from Oxford University in 1576 and by 1580 was one of the most senior Fellows of Balliol College. He was however suspected of Catholic activities and came under surveillance by Government spies. In October 1581 he left the University and made his way to the English College at Rheims, where his arrival is registered for 20 November 1581.

On 3 March, 1583, Pilcher was ordained priest at Laon and he set out for the English Mission on 4 May. At first he worked in Hampshire but according to Father William Warford (who knew him personally) he ranged westwards to cover the whole of the West of England. In 1581, a Government spy reported that Father Pilcher was frequenting the house in Winchester of Lady Mary West, who was well known as a protector of priests. Shortly after this report, the priest was arrested and banished from the country. Father Pilcher returned to Rheims for a short time but was back in England again by January 1586. This time he worked first in the London area where a spy reported his presence in April, but very soon he moved on to his beloved West Country.

In this second period on the English Mission, Father Pilcher preserved his freedom for little more than a year. He was arrested in March 1587 and taken to Dorchester gaol where from the confines of his cell he conducted an active apostolate among his many visitors and among the criminals who shared his captivity. Indeed one of his converts from this time was a notorious robber who was executed at the same time as the priest and who openly professed his Catholic Faith and his repentance for a life of crime.

Father Thomas Pilcher was condemned for his priesthood at the Dorchester Assizes on 21 March 1587 and was executed apparently on the same day as the verdict was given. He suffered exceedingly at the hands of a careless and incompetent executioner.

17. Stephen Rowsham seminary priest

Born in Oxfordshire about 1555
Hanged, drawn and quartered at Gloucester in March, 1587, aged about 32

STEPHEN ROWSHAM was a member of Oriel College, Oxford in 1572, but there is no record that he was ever admitted to a degree. He became a clergyman of the Church of England and served St Mary's parish, Oxford, but was later reconciled to the Catholic Church and entered the English College at Rheims on 23 April, 1581. For the next five months he prepared himself for the priesthood and was ordained at Soissons in late September of the same year.

Father Rowsham left Rheims for the English Mission on 30 April 1582, but was captured as soon as he arrived in his own country. Within three weeks, he was a prisoner in the Tower of London and in August was moved into the special cell known as 'Little Ease', where he spent the next eighteen months in intense suffering but refused to betray his companions. In 1585 he received a sentence of banishment from the kingdom and returned to the English College at Rheims on 8 October.

For the next five months, while he was recuperating from his ordeal in the Tower, Father Rowsham remained in the safety of the English College, but on 7 February 1586 he felt strong enough to make his second attempt to work as a priest in England. This time he evaded capture for about twelve months. His final arrest took place, possibly early in 1587, at the Gloucester home of Mrs Strange, who was well known as a protector of priests.

In prison at Gloucester, Father Rowsham was well treated and allowed to say Mass every day. He was brought to trial at the Lenten Assizes, and, according to Dr Anthony Champney, freely admitted his priesthood. With bitter memories still fresh of the uproar of protest following the cruel butchery of Father John Sandys in the previous August, the authorities took great care to ensure that Father Rowsham was executed with as much humanity as the horrible process of being hanged, drawn and quartered could permit.

18. *John Hambley* seminary priest

Born at St Mabyn near Bodwin, Cornwall about 1560
Hanged, drawn and quartered at Salisbury about March, 1587, aged about 27

JOHN HAMBLEY was brought up as a Protestant but at Christmas 1582 he was given a book written by Father Robert Persons SJ and was so impressed that he ceased to attend the services of the Established Church.

Leaving Cornwall for safety's sake, the young man settled in Smithfield, London, and was reconciled to the Catholic Church by Father John Bollard in the Red Lion Inn at Holborn. On 28 May 1583 John Hambley was received at the English College at Rheims, and on 22 September 1584 he was ordained priest at Laon. He set out for the English Mission on 6 April 1585.

With two companions Father Hambley landed on the coast of East Anglia, and from there went to London where he worked as a priest in Holborn in partnership with his fellow Cornishman, Blessed John Cornelius. In May 1585 he moved to Dorset and made his headquarters in the home of a Catholic farmer, Andrew Munday, near Beauminster. From here he served the Catholics of a large area westwards until, after a year's fruitful activity, he was captured on the road at Crewkerne in Somerset. He was imprisoned at Ilchester, brought to trial at Taunton and there condemned to death.

At this time, his courage seems to have failed him; and, faced with the prospect of a painful death, he expressed some willingness to conform to the State Church. That his gesture fell short of denying his Faith is shown by the fact that he was not released.

Shortly afterwards John Hambley escaped from custody and took refuge with Mrs Browne at Knoyle in the south-west of Wiltshire. Here the pursuivants tracked him down and once more he was on trial for his life. He was examined by John Piers, the Bishop of Salisbury, and wrote a long confession in which he agreed to renounce the Church of Rome and conform to the Church of England. In spite of this, his trial went ahead at the Wiltshire Assizes in Salisbury in Lent 1587 and he was condemned to death. After passing sentence, one of the judges, Sir Thomas Gent, offered the prisoner his life if he would conform fully to the Protestant religion, and Father Hambley accepted the offer.

Next day in court the priest was asked to confirm his renunciation of the Catholic Church, but, as Father William Warford relates, an unknown man came up to the prisoner and handed him a letter. Father Hambley read the letter, burst into tears and openly professed his Catholic Faith. It has never been established what were the contents of this mysterious letter or who wrote it, but Father Warford is quite certain that it was responsible for Father Hambley's change of heart. He went to his death with great faith and renewed courage. And who is to be commended more: the man who never knows fear or the man who knows fear and conquers it?

19. Edmund Sykes seminary priest

Born in Leeds, Yorkshire about 1550
Hanged, drawn and quartered at York on 23 March, 1588, aged about 38

EDMUND SYKES, it would appear, was troubled by sickness even in his youth, and there is evidence that his preparation for the priesthood was impeded by bouts of ill-health. He entered the English College at Rheims on 22 January 1580, was ordained priest on 21 February 1581, and set out for England on 5 June 1581.

A paper written about 1595 and preserved in Grene's Collection F describes how Father Sykes 'lived a very strict and strait life, wandering as a poor pilgrim, and coming to Leeds did help many with his holy life and doctrine', and the same paper goes on to relate that after working on the mission for four years, the priest fell sick with 'an extreme ague' and in this condition fell into the hands of the professional priest-hunter, Arthur Webster.

Father Sykes was taken to York and committed to the notorious Kidcotes, the prisons under Ousebridge, where the damp and cold of the river only increased his sufferings. In his debilitated condition he could not resist the persuasions of his captors and he agreed to attend the Protestant Church. At once, the priest regretted his lapse, but it was too late. Instead of being sentenced to death as a priest, Father Sykes was deported. He was put on board ship at Hull with nine other banished priests, landed at Le Havre and from there made his own way overland to Rheims.

Father Sykes bitterly regretted that he had given in to his captors and denied his Faith. He resolved to spend the rest of his life in penance. He went to Rome to seek absolution and in the Holy City received what he believed was a divine revelation telling him to go back to England where he could receive the martyr's crown.

On 16 June 1586, Father Sykes left Rheims to return to Leeds. Restored in health and spirit he was able to continue his work for about twelve months, but was then betrayed by his own brother while staying in his house near Tanfield in Wensleydale. Once more Father Sykes was taken to York to face trial for his priesthood. The judge taunted the priest about his former weakness and suggested that what he had done once he could do again. Father Sykes was unmoved. 'It was the infirmity of sickness which caused me to go to your service,' he said 'and not for any liking I had of it, the which I have repented and now detest to do it.' (*ibid.*).

Condemned to death, Father Sykes was kept in solitary confinement so that no priest could visit him to administer the sacraments. He prepared himself on his own to receive the crown he had been promised in Rome.

20. Nicholas Garlick seminary priest

Born at Dinting near Glossop, Derbyshire about 1555
Hanged, drawn and quartered at Derby on 24 July, 1588, aged about 33

NICHOLAS GARLICK spent a short time at Oxford University but owing to religious problems had to leave without a degree. A dedicated Catholic, he became a schoolmaster at Tideswell, not far from his place of birth. He entered the English College at Rheims on 22 June 1581, and was ordained priest at Châlons-sur-Marne towards the end of March, 1582. He left for the English Mission on 25 January 1583.

His presence in Staffordshire was noted by a Government spy late in 1584 and soon afterwards he was arrested in London, put into prison and subsequently banished. He was back in Rheims on 17 October 1585, and stayed two days before setting out again for England.

The Douai Diary reports that Father Garlick was in London in April 1586 and then he was sighted by a Government spy during the following September in Hampshire and Dorset. A government list of recusants for March 1588 proclaims his presence in Derbyshire. It was in Derbyshire that Father Garlick was finally arrested. He was staying with Father Robert Ludlam at the safe house of the dedicated Fitzherbert family at Padley when the house was raided by no less a personage than George Talbot, Earl of Shrewsbury and Lord Lieutenant of Derbyshire. The Earl was really searching for Mr John Fitzherbert, but to capture two priests as well was an unexpected bonus.

In prison at Derby, Father Garlick and Father Ludlam met a third captured priest, Father Richard Simpson, and together they were tried, condemned and executed. Today these three priests are widely known and deeply loved as the Padley Martyrs, and there have been public pilgrimages in their honour to Padley Hall since 1898.

21. Robert Ludlam seminary priest

Born in Derbyshire about 1551
Hanged, drawn and quartered at Derby on 24 July, 1588, aged about 37

ROBERT LUDLAM matriculated in the University of Oxford in 1575, but as a Catholic experienced religious difficulties and left without a degree. He entered the English College at Rheims on 25 November 1580, and was ordained priest towards the end of

September 1581. He set out for the English Mission on 30 April 1582, and preserved his freedom for six years.

He was said to have been 'beloved by all that loved the Catholic Church' and to have done much good in the country 'for that he did much travel'. But these remarks by an unknown contemporary (in Grene's Collection F) shed little light on the activities of a priest who must have lived even more secretly than many of his priestly colleagues. Perhaps there is a clue in the phrase 'that he did much travel'. Certainly to have evaded capture for six years was a great achievement for a priest in the 1580s.

Father Ludlam was arrested in the same circumstances as related for Father Robert Garlick and in his company and that of Father Robert Simpson he was brought to trial, condemned and executed.

22. Richard Simpson seminary priest

Born at Well near Bedale, Yorkshire about 1553
Hanged, drawn and quartered at Derby on 24 July, 1588, aged about 35

THE SECOND DOUAI DIARY records that Richard Simpson had suffered a long imprisonment in York before reaching the English College at Douai in May 1577. He arrived as the College was preparing to move to Rheims and the consequent disorganisation had its effect on the keeping of records. Hence all that is known about Simpson is that he was ordained priest at Brussels in the same year as his arrival at the College and that he set out for the English Mission in September. His seminary course therefore lasted a mere matter of three or four months.

In England, Father Simpson seems to have worked in Derbyshire. There is some confusion about identification because there were in fact several Father Simpsons, but there is no doubt that Father Richard Simpson was arrested in the Peak District in January 1588. An anonymous document of 1588 in Grene's Collection F gives the additional information that Father Simpson was betrayed by a stranger who pretended to be a Catholic and then denounced the priest in Derby.

At his trial, Father Simpson was condemned to death; but weakness overcame him, and he yielded to the persuasions of his captors, giving them an undertaking that he would listen to a Protestant sermon or go to one of their services. His surrender was not complete; it did not satisfy the judge. He was not released but remanded for a second trial. It was while Father Simpson was waiting for this second trial that Father Garlick and Father Ludlam were arrested at Padley and all three priests were imprisoned together. If Father Simpson was still wavering he was certainly strengthened and encouraged by the presence, words and example of his brother priests. 'Mr Simpson was reclaimed by Mr Garlick and Mr Ludlam', wrote Bishop Challoner in 1741.

Father Simpson deeply regretted whatever weakness he may have shown and he spent the rest of his days doing penance. On the scaffold, he embraced the ladder, kissed the steps and died bravely. When his body was cut down be was seen to be wearing the hair shirt of a penitent.

23. Robert Sutton seminary priest

Born at Burton on Trent, Staffordshire in 1545
Hanged, drawn and quartered at Stafford on 27 July, 1588, aged 43

ROBERT SUTTON was the son of a carpenter. At the age of sixteen he won a scholarship to Oxford University, and the Buttery Books of Christ Church show that he was in residence from 1561 until 1571. Having proceeded MA he took orders in the Anglican Church and became Rector of Lutterworth in Leicestershire, where he stayed until 1576.

While Rector of this Parish, Robert Sutton was much influenced by his younger brother, William, who had become a Catholic and a student at the English College at Douai. Robert decided to follow his brother's example and according to Father John Gerard SJ he announced his conversion to his assembled parishioners and apologised for the errors he had taught them for the previous five years.

Robert Sutton was accompanied by Abraham, another of his brothers, when he journeyed across the seas to Douai. Both were admitted to the English College on 23 March 1577, and were just in time to attend William's ordination to the priesthood. Robert and Abraham were themselves ordained on 23 February 1578, and together they left for the English Mission on 19 March.

Father Robert Sutton seems to have worked as a priest in the Staffordshire area and evaded arrest for ten years. He was finally caught at Stafford on 18 July 1588, in the company of seven lay Catholics. Brother H. Foley SJ says that the arrest took place while the priest was visiting the Catholic prisoners in Stafford gaol, but Father John Gerard SJ places it in a private house and Thomas Worswick, writing before 1619, claims that Father Sutton was actually saying Mass when he was apprehended.

The trial took place at the Stafford Summer Assizes of 1588, when the laymen were found guilty of harbouring the priest but were allowed to pay for their pardons. Father Robert Sutton was sentenced to death for his priesthood and then executed in a particularly cruel manner.

24. Henry Webley layman

Born in Gloucester about 1558
Hanged at Mile End, London, on 28 August, 1588, aged about 30

IT WAS the usual practice in the 1580s for a Catholic layman to be attached to each seminary priest as his guide and protector, and such was the responsibility of Henry Webley for Father William Dean. Both were arrested in April 1586 in Chichester harbour on a ship about to sail for France. The circumstances would suggest that both were under pressure from the pursuivants and that they were seeking safety overseas for a time.

Official prison lists show that Henry Webley was taken to the Marshalsea prison in London and he is described as a recusant and prisoner for matter of religion. There is also a note that he was 'neither wealthy nor wise but very arrogant'. For two years, Henry Webley lingered quietly in prison without being brought to trial and he might have stayed there undisturbed for the rest of his life had there not been a sudden upsurge of anti-Catholic feelings throughout the country in July 1588 as the Spanish Armada was decisively defeated and Englishmen expressed their joy and relief by attacking the Catholics whom they believed quite erroneously were the friends of Spain.

In response to this public outcry, the Privy Council commissioned a London lawyer, John Puckering, to draw up a list of Catholic prisoners so that 'they might be proceeded with according to the law and as the quality of their offences deserved'. The rough notes for this list have been preserved and were printed in 1908 in the Catholic Record Society's volume V. Henry Webley's name appears in the first section of this paper. He is described as one who had been reconciled to the Catholic Church and therefore by implication guilty of high treason, but a later note by Lord Burghley, the Queen's Chief Minister alters the charge to harbouring a priest in contravention of the 1585 Act.

The trial took place on the 26 August 1588, and Henry Webley was in good company. Sixteen other Catholics were charged at the same time. Three recanted but all the others were found guilty and sentenced to death, and all have now been beatified by the Church. Six of them were priests: William Dean, William Gunter, Robert Morton, Thomas Holford, James Claxton and Richard Leigh; one was a cleric, Thomas Felton; and six were laymen: Hugh More, Edward Shelley, Richard Martin, John Roche, Richard Flower and Henry Webley. By the Queen's mercy, the sentence of death by being hanged, drawn and quartered was reduced to simple hanging for all these martyrs.

On 28 August 1588, Henry Webley accompanied his priest on their last journey. He and Father William Dean were taken in a cart to Mile End Green and there they were both hanged.

25. Richard Flower

layman

Born at Anglesey, Wales about 1566
Hanged at Tyburn, London on 30 August, 1588, aged about 22

RICHARD FLOWER'S real name was Lloyd but he is also known as Floyd, Flewet and Gray. The name Flower first appeared in Stowe's Annals of 1605 either as an error or a misprint but it was then passed through the Catalogues of Worthington and Chalcedon until it was accepted by Bishop Challoner.

It has been suggested that Flower belonged to a group of young Catholics who came together in London with the purpose of helping their priests, not merely by providing protection but by collecting alms for their support from their fellow Catholics. Thomas Dodwell, the Government spy, referred to Richard Flower in February 1584 as one of 'the chiefest relievers of priests' (Foley's *Records* VI, 727).

Richard Flower was arrested on 14 March 1588, and a copy of his indictment is still in existence (Catholic Record Society V, 164). This states that his crime was that in the parish of St Dunstan in the West, he 'received, comforted, aided and maintained' a priest, Father William Horner. A contemporary writer maintains that all he did was to give the priest some supper (*Troubles of our Catholic Forefathers*, III p.33). For this charity to the priest, Richard Flower was condemned at Newgate Assizes on 26 August 1588, and was one of the thirteen Catholics sentenced to death in the aftermath of the Spanish Armada.

On the day of execution, Richard Flower was carried in a cart with four other men from Newgate to Tyburn. All along the way they sang hymns of joy and the priest among them, Father Richard Leigh, gave his blessing indiscriminately to his companions and the throngs of people who watched. On the scaffold they were joined by St Margaret Ward who was to die with them.

According to Father Henry Walpole SJ (*Acts of the English Martyrs*, p.306), Father Leigh spoke at great length to the spectators and then demanded time for prayer before the hangman did his duty and Richard Flower paid with his life for his devotion to God's priests.

26. *Edward Burden* seminary priest

Born in County Durham (Stockton on Tees?) about 1540
Hanged, drawn and quartered at York about 29 November, 1588, aged about 48

IT IS UNLIKELY that Edward Burden was a Catholic when he entered Corpus Christi College, Oxford, in August 1558. He became a Fellow in 1561 and proceeded MA in December 1566. These were the years when the influence of St Edmund Campion SJ was strong in the University, and the Rev James Clayton, writing in 1914, has referred to the Campionists or 'the young men who became Campion's pupils and who were such ardent followers of their master, that they imitated not only his phrases but his gait'.

With or without the influence of Campion, Edward Burden became a Catholic, and was already over forty when he entered the English College at Rheims on 24 June 1583. He was ordained to the priesthood at Soissons on 13 June 1584, but ill-health prevented his immediate return to England. Eventually he set out for his Mission on 22 May 1586, and based himself in Yorkshire. He may have lived in York but at his trial he was accused of indulging in priestly activities around Ripon.

The rigours of the life of a missionary priest were too much for Father Burden's strength. A contemporary, probably Father Richard Holtby SJ, gives the information that he was suffering from tuberculosis (*Acts of the English Martyrs*, p.328). Early in 1588, therefore, he tried to hide himself away for a much-needed rest in the quiet hamlet of Skinningrove on the north-east coast of Yorkshire. It was here while out walking that he chanced to meet a Mr John Constable, who became suspicious, questioned him closely and then arrested him.

Father Burden was taken to York where he appeared before the Council and was imprisoned in the Castle. In the harsh conditions of prison his sickness returned and when he was summoned to meet his judges he had to rise from his sick bed. He was questioned as to where he had worked as a priest and asked to name those who had helped him, but his reply was straightforward: 'You enquire things of me for no good end and therefore I will not answer' (Foley, *Records SJ*, p.737).

Father Edward Burden was found guilty of being a priest and was condemned to death. On the scaffold he tried to speak to the spectators as was his right but they shouted him down with cries of, 'Despatch him; for he is able to do much hurt'. He died a brave death at the Knavesmire, York, in 1588, but there is some uncertainty about the precise day.

27. *William Lampley* layman

Born (possibly) in Gloucester; date unknown
Hanged, drawn and quartered at Gloucester in 1588

WILLIAM LAMPLEY, a glover by trade and a very poor man lived a humble life in the city of Gloucester and his activities have made little impact on historical records. That he is accepted officially by the Church as one of the Blessed Martyrs is due mainly to the strength of Catholic tradition. He was recognised by his Catholic contemporaries as a true martyr and this belief is reflected by the appearance of his name in no fewer than eight of the early Catalogues of Martyrs from Worthington's first list of 1608 to the authoritative Paris Catalogue of about 1628.

Father John Morris SJ, in *Troubles of our Catholic Forefathers* (III, 41), has used a paper of about 1592 in Grene's Collection E to provide a little detail about this rather obscure martyr. His offence was that he had broken the Statute of 1581 by 'persuading' a member of his family to become a Catholic. At Gloucester Assizes he was convicted on the evidence of one witness, who, moreover, was possessed of an unsavoury reputation. The judge, Sir Roger Manwood, condemned William Lampley to death, but then used every endeavour to prevent the sentence being carried out. He assured the prisoner that if only he would attend the Protestant church for one service he would be released at once. Lampley refused the offer. The judge renewed his entreaties, and was so anxious to save this poor man's life that he sent his own friends and members of his family as well as court officials and local Protestant clergymen to visit him and use their best endeavours to convince him that he should accept the judge's invitation and renounce his

Catholic faith. William Lampley never wavered for a moment and prepared himself for death.

The execution took place at Gloucester in 1588 and not even the day of the month is recorded. The document used by Father Morris simply states that 'they ended him as butcherly and bloodily as ever they did any' (*ibid.*) and this is taken to mean death by being hanged, drawn and quartered. William Lampley may have been a very insignificant man in the eyes of the world but he had the extraordinary courage and faith of a Christian martyr.

28. George Nichols seminary priest

Born at Oxford about 1550
Hanged, drawn and quartered at Oxford on 5 July, 1589, aged about 39

GEORGE NICHOLS graduated from Brasenose College, Oxford, in 1571 and worked for some years as an assistant master at St Paul's School, London, before becoming a Catholic. He entered the English College at Rheims in November 1581, was ordained priest in Rheims Cathedral on 24 September 1583, and departed for the English Mission sometime in 1584.

Father Nichols worked as a priest in his home district of Oxford. In 1587 he secretly visited the prison and effected the reconciliation of the notorious highwayman, Harcourt Taverner, who before dying on the scaffold for his criminal offences openly professed his Catholic Faith and expressed his penitence.

In 1589 the Privy Council, hearing from a spy that there was much Catholic activity around Oxford, ordered a special search for priests. The Constable of Oxford lead a party of pursuivants in a sudden raid on the Catherine Wheel Inn, which was reputed to be a Catholic headquarters. In the Inn they found Father George Nichols and another priest, Father Richard Yaxley, as well as the vital evidence of a quantity of mass vestments.

The two priests were arrested together with two laymen, Humphrey Pritchard and Thomas Belson. All four were questioned next day before the Court of the Chancellor of the University and Father George Nichols admitted that he was a priest, but as the Privy Council was closely involved in this affair the prisoners were sent to

London. Once more they were questioned and attempts were made to force them to give information. Father Nichols withstood the torture and resisted all the pressure that was brought to bear on him to incriminate his friends, but did not deny that he was a priest.

The whole party was sent back to Oxford for trial. They appeared at the Summer Assizes with Sir Francis Knollys holding a watching brief for the Privy Council, and all were condemned to death. On the scaffold, Father George Nichols was prevented from addressing the crowd but he made a brief profession of faith and was the first to die.

29. Richard Yaxley seminary priest

Born in Boston, Lincolnshire about 1560
Hanged, drawn and quartered at Oxford on 5 July, 1589, aged about 29

RICHARD YAXLEY entered the English College at Rheims in August 1582, and was ordained priest in Rheims Cathedral on 21 September 1585. He set out for the English Mission on 28 January 1586. At first he stayed with Father Robert Dibdale at Mr Edmund Peckham's house at Denham, Buckinghamshire, and he was involved in the exorcisms which were taking place there. He then moved on to the Oxford district where he worked with Father George Nichols until both priests were arrested when the Catherine Wheel Inn was raided by pursuivants in 1589.

Father Yaxley did not immediately admit his priesthood, and it was only when both were being tortured in London that he gave the authorities this information. He was then removed to the Tower of London and orders were given by the Privy Council that nobody was to visit him except Richard Topcliffe, the notorious torturer.

With his three companions (as related in the account of Father George Nichols), Father Yaxley was brought back to Oxford for trial and there condemned to death for his priesthood. He followed Father Nichols on the scaffold and watched him die. Then he embraced the body of the dead priest and asked for his prayers before submitting himself calmly to the executioner.

30. Thomas Belson layman

Born at Ixhill Lodge, Brill, Buckinghamshire about 1565
Hanged at Oxford on 5 July, 1589, aged about 24

THOMAS BELSON came from a strong Catholic family and in his youth had persisted in his firm refusal to attend the services of the Established Church. Possibly for his own safety he was sent overseas, and in 1584 he was at the English College in Rheims. He did not pursue studies for the priesthood, however, and returned to England in April of the same year.

In London, as an energetic Catholic in his early twenties, he was soon in trouble with the authorities. The Tower Bills show that Thomas Belson was a prisoner in the Tower from 24 June 1585, until 30 September 1586, and the Government Prison Lists show that he was still there on 30 November and that he was to be banished from the realm 'for conveying intelligence between Bridges the priest and others beyond the seas and some in this realm by unknown means'.

By the spring of 1589 Thomas Belson had returned from banishment, and he was arrested with Father George Nichols and Father Richard Yaxley when the Catherine Wheel Inn, Oxford, was raided by the pursuivants. With the priests, he was taken to London and questioned by the Privy Council. He declined the invitation to disclose any Catholic information, saying boldly, 'I am a Catholic gentleman'.

Thomas Belson was sentenced to death at Oxford Assizes and on the scaffold embraced the dead bodies of the two martyred priests and remarked to the bystanders that he was glad to appear before God in such good company.

31. *Humphrey Pritchard* layman

Born in Wales, date unknown
Hanged at Oxford on 5 July, 1589, age unknown

HUMPHREY PRITCHARD first appears in Catholic records as the inn-servant who opened the door to the pursuivants when they raided the Catherine Wheel Inn at Oxford. He was immediately arrested and when the priests, Father George Nichols and Father Richard Yaxley, were found and the evidence of the Mass vestments discovered, Pritchard was one of the four taken into custody for further questioning. Before the Vice-Chancellor of Oxford in the Chancellor's Court, Humphrey Pritchard freely admitted that he was a Catholic and was therefore taken with the others to London to be questioned further by the Privy Council.

Perhaps the authorities never discovered the full importance of Humphrey Pritchard. He was much more than a simple serving man in an inn. He was the trusted helper and adviser of the pious Catholic widow who owned the establishment and organised it as a powerful centre of activity for the missionary priests. Bishop Richard Challoner has described Humphrey Pritchard as 'a plain, honest, and well-meaning soul, and a great servant of God, who for twelve years had done signal service to the poor, afflicted, persecuted Catholics in those evil days'.

Humphrey Pritchard was condemned to death at the Oxford Assizes in 1589 for harbouring the priests. On the scaffold, he watched his three companions die; and when his own turn came, he accepted the rope with a smile on his face, professed his Faith and was then hanged.

32. *William Spenser* seminary priest

Born at Gisburn, West Yorkshire, about 1555
Hanged, drawn and quartered at York on 24 September, 1589, aged about 34

WILLIAM SPENSER was a personal friend of Father William Warford SJ, who spent eight years with him at Oxford University and then accompanied him across the seas to the English

College at Rheims. In his extensive writings, Father Warford has recorded many details of the life, mission and death of his friend and these have been preserved in the Westminster Archives and printed in the *Acts of the English Martyrs* (pp.273-278).

According to Father Warford, William Spenser's parents had conformed or pretended to conform to the State Church, but they sent their son to be educated by his uncle, the Reverend Mr Horn, at Cornwall, near Chipping Norton in Oxfordshire. This clergyman was very much a Catholic at heart and Miss Enid Dinnis has suggested (*The Pope's Men*, 1924) that the boy was sent to him to be secretly educated as a Catholic. Certainly when he entered Trinity College, Oxford, in 1572, William Spenser was keenly interested in Catholic affairs and gave the impression to many people that he had already been reconciled. Such could not have been the case as his formal progress through University to Fellow of his College and Master of Arts depended on his conformity to the Church of England.

In 1582 the religious pressures of the University became too much and William Spenser moved to the English College at Rheims, where his arrival is recorded for 2 November 1582. A few days later he was formally reconciled to the Church and within the year he was ordained priest on 24 September 1583.

Father Spenser's first concern as a priest was for his mother and father and in an open field near their home he received them into the Church. Next, he visited Oxfordshire to reconcile his uncle, Mr Horne, who resigned his Church of England benefice and retired to live with a Catholic gentleman. After this, as Father Warford has written, 'he began more freely and boldly to expose himself to danger and to work more earnestly in order to help souls'. His compassion was aroused by the wretched plight of the Catholic prisoners in York Castle and in order to provide them with Mass and the sacraments he made himself a voluntary prisoner in their midst. He devised his own hiding-place in the Castle and managed to move in and out freely without disturbing the guards.

On 1 August 1589, Father Spenser's apostolate of five years was ended. He was arrested with his lay protector, Robert Hardesty, on the road near Ripon and both were taken to York, charged before the Council of the North and condemned to death. Father Spenser spent his last moments on the scaffold shaking his head in vehement disagreement with the theological proposals of the attendant Anglican clergyman; and then, as one of the Catholic witnesses has stated, 'he took his death merrily'.

33. Robert Hardesty layman

Born in Yorkshire; date unknown
Hanged at York on 24 September, 1589; age unknown

ROBERT HARDESTY was the young Catholic layman who was looking after Father William Spenser when both were arrested near Ripon on 1 August 1589. The unknown author of a paper of about 1592 (in Grene's Collection E), gives some detail about Hardesty's imprisonment in York Castle. 'He gave himself much to contemplation and prayer, desiring always to be solitary, saying his beads every day twelve time, besides other devotions'. Then wishing to go to confession to Father Spenser, who was in the same prison but a different cell, he made his confession to the priest through a hole in the wall. As he expressed his sorrow for his sins he 'began to howl, lament, roar and cry out so mightily and so loud that he was heard all over the prison'. His fellow prisoners tried to calm his frenzy and laid him on a bed and after three hours he recovered from what he and his companions believed to be an extraordinary mystical experience.

Robert Hardesty was brought to trial before the Council of the North and charged with harbouring a priest. This he could vehemently deny for, in order to allay suspicions, he had been walking a full furlong ahead of the priest at the time of the arrest. At this stage the judge, Mr Laurence Meares, altered the charge, and according to the unknown author of another paper preserved by Father Christopher Grene, (c. 1595, Collection F) brought in the Keeper of the Prison, Mr Anthony Ellis, to testify that Hardesty had helped the Catholic prisoners (among whom were several priests) by supplying them with bacon, cheese and venison. On this evidence

Robert Hardesty was sentenced to death, and he who had shared the dangers of Father William Spenser's priestly life now shared his martyrdom.

34. Nicholas Horner layman

Born in Ripon, Yorkshire; date unknown
Hanged in Smithfield, London on 4 March, 1590; age unknown

NICHOLAS HORNER was a devout Catholic who had spent most of his life working in York as a tailor. Advanced in years and suffering from a diseased leg he travelled to London about 1588 in search of medical treatment. Father Robert Persons SJ referred to him as 'a very holy old man'; St Henry Walpole SJ called him 'Father Horner' in tribute to his years.

In London Nicholas Horner was soon arrested and his name appears on the Government Prison Lists for 30 September 1588 (see Catholic Record Society, vol. II p.283), as one who, faced with the 'bloody question', would not swear to take the Queen's side against the hypothetical papal invasion. In Newgate prison, Nicholas Horner was placed in a special cell (called Limbo by the Catholics) and irons were put on his legs. Inevitably the condition of his diseased leg deteriorated and he had to suffer the painful ordeal of having it amputated.

After a year's convalescence in prison Nicholas Horner was released and was able to return to his lodgings in Smithfield where he re-started his work as a tailor. His period of freedom was brief. Richard Topcliffe searched the house and claimed that he had found evidence of the presence of priests. Once more Nicholas Horner was taken to prison and this time was tortured by Topcliffe himself. But an old man who could pray calmly while his leg was being amputated was not likely to betray his priests even under Topcliffe's torture (*Acts of the English Martyrs*, p.227).

Nicholas Horner was brought to trial and found guilty of harbouring priests. He was hanged outside his own lodgings and a sign was displaced over the gallows, 'For treason and favouring foreign invasion'.

35. *Alexander Blake* layman

Born in London (?); date unknown
Hanged at Gray's Inn Lane, London, on 4 March, 1590

ALEXANDER BLAKE has been described by his contemporaries as 'a poor man that kept lodgings' and as 'a poor man that was an ostler in Gray's Inn Lane'. He was obviously well known to the Catholic community in London but the details of his humble life have not been recorded. It is known that he was hanged outside the inn at which he worked in Gray's Inn Lane on the same day as Father Christopher Bales was hanged, drawn and quartered in Fleet Street and Mr Nicholas Horner was hanged at Smithfield, and a Government tract of 1590 (re-printed in the Catholic Record Society's vol. XXXII, p.428) links the three executions by claiming that Mr Horner and Mr Blake were hanged 'for secret harbouring, receiving and denying this priest'.

Yet despite the meagre written evidence there is no doubt at all that Alexander Blake was accepted as a true martyr by the Catholics of his time and his name appears in nine Catalogues of Martyrs between 1594 and the most authoritative Catalogue of Chalcedon in 1628.

36. *Edmund Duke* seminary priest

Born in Kent in 1563
Hanged, drawn and quartered at Durham on 27 May, 1590, aged 27

EDMUND DUKE entered the English College at Rheims on 3 March 1583 and received the sacrament of confirmation there two months later. He was later moved to the Venerable English College in Rome where his admission is recorded for 20 October 1584, and he was ordained priest in the Lateran Basilica on 3 September 1589. Immediately after his ordination, Father Duke returned to the English College at Rheims where he joined the three young priests, Father Richard Hill, Father John Hogg and Father Richard Holiday, who were waiting for a favourable opportunity to cross the seas to England.

Alarming reports were reaching the College from England. Too many priests were being arrested as soon as they landed on the coast. Government spies and priest-catchers were so active and so successful that much of the missionary organisation was in disarray. Prudence demanded a pause before any more missionaries were sent. The four young priests waited at Rheims for six long months before it was decided that the persecution seemed to be lessening and permission was given for them to attempt the crossing to South Shields on the north east coast.

By this time the priests were well informed and well trained to make use of every safety measure devised by Father Richard Holtby SJ and Father John Mush for the north eastern counties of England. Their instructions were clear. When the ship docked at South Shields they would be met by a Catholic messenger who would conduct them to a safe house organised by Mrs Ursula Taylor. They would be supplied with food, clothes and money by Mr Laurence Kellam and then Mr George Errington would lead them by secret ways to the mission headquarters at Grosmont on the North Yorkshire Moors. Unfortunately what the priests did not know was that the safe house had just been raided by the pursuivants and that the whole courier system had broken down. Nobody met them on the quay at South Shields. They could find no friendly Catholic at all. They decided that the best they could do was to find their own way south to Yorkshire.

Their enterprise was doomed to failure. They had to cross the whole county of Durham where almost everyone was on the alert to recognise and capture Catholic priests. Four young priests in a group on the open road had no chance at all. It was while they were resting at Coxhoe near Durham that they were accosted and arrested. They were taken to Durham, tried and condemned to death. At Dryburn, then just outside Durham, Father Edmund Duke and his companions, Father Richard Hill, Father John Hogg and Father Richard Holiday were executed before they had even begun their missionary apostolate.

37. Richard Hill seminary priest

Born in Yorkshire, possibly in 1565
Hanged, drawn and quartered at Durham on 27 May, 1590, aged possibly 25

RICHARD HILL entered the English College at Rheims on 15 May 1587. He was ordained priest at Laon on 23 September 1589. He was one of the group of four priests whose martyrdom is described in section 36 on Father Edmund Duke.

38. John Hogg seminary priest

Born in Ugthorpe, Cleveland, possibly in 1565
Hanged, drawn and quartered at Durham on 27 May, 1590, possibly aged 25

JOHN HOGG arrived at the English College at Rheims on 15 October 1587. He was ordained priest at Laon on 23 September 1589. He was one of the group of four priests whose martyrdom is described in section 36 on Father Edmund Duke.

39. Richard Holiday seminary priest

Born in Yorkshire, possibly in 1565
Hanged, drawn and quartered at Durham on 27 May, 1590, possibly aged 25

RICHARD HOLIDAY entered the English College at Rheims on 6 September 1584. He was ordained priest at Laon on 23 September 1589. He was one of the group of four priests whose martyrdom is described in section 36 on Father Edmund Duke.

40. *Robert Thorpe* seminary priest

Born in Yorkshire; date unknown
Hanged, drawn and quartered at York on 31 May, 1591

ROBERT THORPE arrived at the English College in Rheims on 1 May 1584, and was ordained priest in Rheims Cathedral on 6 April 1585. For the next six years he worked as a travelling priest in the East Riding of Yorkshire. He was a regular visitor to the Catholic community at Osgodby Hall and Lady Grace Babthorpe has described him as a man 'of low stature, of infirm health, of mediocre learning, but of great devotion and piety'.

He was captured in the house of Mr Thomas Watkinson at Menthorpe, a very small village close to Howden. His quiet entry into the village on the previous evening had been noted and reported to Mr Gates, the Justice of the Peace at Howden. The house was raided in the early hours of Palm Sunday, 28 March 1591, and all the occupants taken to prison in York (*Troubles of our Catholic Forefathers*, III p.179ff.)

For some unknown reason Richard Topcliffe took a special interest in this case (Catholic Record Society, vol. V, p. 201). The insignificant Father Thorpe was summoned from York to London for a special session with the torturer and Topcliffe accompanied the priest back to York and sat with the Council of the North for the trial. Father Thorpe was found guilty and executed at the same time as his host, Mr Watkinson. 'He died', wrote Father Anthony Champney in 1618, 'because he was a priest'.

41. *Thomas Watkinson* layman

Born at Menthorpe, Hemingbrough, Yorkshire; date unknown
Hanged at York on 31 May, 1591

THOMAS WATKINSON was a typical Howdenshire Catholic of his time. He was no longer a young man but his house at Menthorpe was well known to priests who visited him. The Act Books for the Court of High Commission in York show that Watkinson was a persistent offender on religious matters. He was charged on 16 January 1581 with 'absenting himself from the church' and made another appearance on 24 April 1587. Despite his age, he resisted all attempts to force him to conform.

On Palm Sunday, 28 March 1591, when Father Robert Thorpe was arrested in his house, Thomas Watkinson was also taken into custody. Charged before the Council of the North in York with the capital offence of harbouring a priest, he did not hesitate and informed his judges 'I received him as the messenger and the servant of God for my soul's sake'. On receiving his sentence of death, he referred again to his priest visitors and assured the Court that 'if I were in place again, I would receive more than I ever did and now I wish that I had received them more often' (Foley, *Records SJ*, III, 746).

On the day of his execution he attended Father Thorpe's Mass in prison, and then, on the way to the Knavesmire, bade farewell to his sons and daughters and commended them all to God. On the scaffold, Richard Topcliffe offered him 'his life and his lands, if he would become a good subject and go to the church', but as Father Richard Holtby SJ relates, 'he cheerfully refused, choosing rather to be a king in heaven than to live a miserable subject and bondslave to sin in the world, and so embraced his crown'.

42. Montford Scott seminary priest

Born in Suffolk about 1550
Hanged, drawn and quartered in London on 1 July, 1591, aged about 41

MONTFORD SCOTT was from a wealthy East Anglian family and in his youth was an active Catholic. Because of his religion, he had to leave Trinity Hall, Cambridge without a degree, and in the early 1570s his name is included in a List of Recusants in Suffolk (Catholic Record Society, vol. LIII, p.108).

In 1574 Montford Scott was at the English College, Douai. On 10 December 1576, while still a subdeacon, he interrupted his studies to accompany Father Dominic Vaughan to England. Both were soon arrested in Essex and the Privy Council described them as 'wandering from place to place within this realm' in order to 'maliciously seduce Her Majesty's people from the truth and doctrine of the Gospel' (*Acts of the Privy Council*, IX, 255). Montford Scott spent only a short time in prison and then returned to Douai where he was ordained priest in June 1577. He came to England two weeks later to begin a missionary career which was to last for fourteen years.

Father Scott's progress round the country and his activities are well-documented from official Government sources. In 1578 he was arrested in Cambridge, and the Ecclesiastical High Commission ordered that he be sent to London 'with the books, letters, writings and other trash' found on him. He was examined, released on bail and disappeared. In 1580, a spy reported him as being 'about Kent', and in 1582 or 1583 another spy claimed that he was in the city of London. In 1584 the Government launched a massive search in the north of England, and in February of that year the Queen herself ordered a special search in the North Riding of Yorkshire. The elusive Father Scott was not discovered. In April 1584, Father Scott was charged in Norwich with 'distributing divers hallowed beads' and 'saying of divers Masses' in the latter half of the previous year, but the court proceedings took place in the absence of the accused. Nor did he appear when cited before the Court of the Queen's Bench in London and was officially declared an outlaw in June 1585.

For the next five years Father Scott continued his priestly work out of sight of the authorities, and they only caught up with him in December 1590 when he was arrested in the house of Mr William Killbeck near Horncastle in Lincolnshire. The priest was taken to London, to the King's Bench prison, where he audaciously used the opportunity to reconcile to the Catholic Church a fellow prisoner, Evan Lloyd (Catholic Record Society, vol. LX, p.46). He made an attempt to bribe his way out of prison by paying £20 to a man named Baker, but by this time both Richard Topcliffe and Justice Richard Young were determined that he should not escape and he was soon re-arrested.

Father Montford Scott was brought to trial at the same time as Father George Beesley at the Newgate Sessions in London in June

1591. Both men admitted that they were in fact priests and both refused to indulge in any religious bargaining. They were executed together in Fleet Street.

43. George Beesley seminary priest

Born at Goosnargh, Preston, Lancashire in 1563
Hanged, drawn and quartered in London on 1 July, 1591, aged 28

GEORGE BEESLEY entered the English College at Rheims some time before September 1583. He was ordained priest on 14 March 1587, but did not set out for the English Mission until 2 November 1588. His coming to England was reported to Sir Francis Walsingham by a spy in Paris, but inspite of this information, Father Beesley was able to work as a priest for two years.

At first he stayed in the London area and a paper (SP 12/243 93) in the Public Record Office states that he had secretly officiated in the Marshalsea Prison at the wedding of a Catholic prisoner, Richard Webster. He then moved north and would seem to have worked at different times in the Durham, Lancaster and York districts. During the summer of 1590 he was once more near London, and, while staying at the house of John and Margaret Gage at Haling in Surrey, he was arrested and committed to the Tower of London.

Father George Beesley was one of those unfortunate prisoners in whom Richard Topcliffe took a special interest. He was kept in solitary confinement, threatened with the horrors of Little Ease and most cruelly tortured. When Dr Anthony Champney saw him later he said that he had suffered so much that his friends could scarcely recognise him.

At the end of June 1591, Father Beesley was transferred to Newgate Prison for his trial. With Father Montford Scott he was sentenced to death and both priests died together in Fleet Street.

44. William Pike layman

Born in the county of Dorset; date unknown
Hanged, drawn and quartered at Dorchester in 1591

WILLIAM PIKE worked as a carpenter or wheelwright in the hamlet of West Moors, which is in the parish of West Parley in the county of Dorset, and was converted to the Catholic Church when he first met Father Thomas Pilcher about two years before the priest was martyred at Dorchester in 1587. As a Catholic, William Pike was arrested, put in Dorchester Prison and then tried at the Assizes. In court he was questioned about his views on the spiritual supremacy of the Queen and he refused to take the oath. This in itself was not a capital offence but it certainly prejudiced his case. When asked if he would conform to the Established Church he replied with some heat that he could not do so because such conduct would be unbecoming for a spiritual son of Father Pilcher. And according to Father William Warford (*Acts of the English Martyrs*, p.266), he then went on to explain that Father Pilcher was 'the holy priest of God and true Martyr for Christ, who taught me the truth of the Catholic Faith'. These words were an admission that he had been reconciled to Rome by Father Pilcher and that in itself was a capital offence.

William Pike was condemned to death but the exact date of his execution is not recorded. His manner of death was to be hanged, drawn and quartered. He suffered bravely and was immediately recognised by his contemporaries as a true Martyr and is included in all the principal Catalogues of Martyrs.

45. Thomas Pormort seminary priest

Born at Little Limber, Brocklesby, Lincolnshire, in 1560
Hanged, drawn and quartered in St Paul's Churchyard, London on 20 February, 1592, aged 32

THOMAS PORMORT was baptised in the Church of England and had the Anglican Archbishop of Canterbury, John Whitgift, as his godfather. He studied at Trinity College, Cambridge, but left the University without a degree, and it was as a convert to Catholicism that he entered the English College at Rheims in January 1581. Four months later he moved on to the Venerable English College in Rome, where his arrival is recorded for 8 May 1581. He was ordained priest in the Lateran Basilica on 23 August 1587.

At this time, according to the Register of the Venerable English College, Father Pormort's health was not considered good enough for his immediate return to England, and he took service with the Welshman, Owen Lewis, who was Bishop of Cassano in the kingdom of Naples. Father Robert Persons SJ is less kind; he says Thomas Pormort had been 'somewhat troublesome in College' and was sent to Bishop Lewis at his own request (*Venerabile* XX, p.219).

In December 1590 Father Pormort came to London. His journey from Flushing was arranged for him by Father Henry Walpole SJ and in the city he first stayed with St Robert Southwell, who provided him with clothes and money and introduced him to his Catholic friends. Father Pormort's active apostolate lasted only about six months. In July 1591 he reconciled to the Church a haberdasher named John Bowis, and shortly after this reconciliation he was recognised in a London street by an apostate priest, William Tedder (*Venerabile* XX, p.219). He was arrested, taken to the Bridewell prison, and then, possibly because of his relationship with Archbishop John Whitgift, was claimed by Richard Topcliffe for special questioning. Topcliffe was convinced that he could make Father Pormort renounce the Catholic Church and that he could extract from him incriminating evidence about the London Catholics. For these purposes he used torture, and Bishop Richard Challoner, relying on the evidence of Dr Anthony Champney (c. 1618), has described how 'he was several times cruelly racked' so that 'his body was all disjointed and he suffered a rupture' (*Missionary Priests*, 1741, p.281).

Topcliffe also used persuasions, and Father Pormort himself has left a detailed account of these conversations, (Catholic Record Society, vol. V, p.210). He makes very serious charges against Topcliffe, who promised him his life and ecclesiastical preferment if he would conform to the Established Church, and then in order to prove that he had the power to fulfill these promises, boasted in a scandalous manner about the intimate relationship which he claimed to enjoy with the Queen.

All Topcliffe's efforts were in vain. Father Pormort refused to conform and refused to betray his companions. He was therefore brought to trial at the Newgate Sessions on 18 February 1592, and charged with his priesthood. He was charged also with the reconciliation of Mr John Bowis, who by this time had given up his Catholic religion and was prepared to give evidence against the priest who had received him into the Church. Father Pormort was sentenced to death, and the cruelty of Topcliffe pursued him even to the scaffold, for by Topcliffe's decision the execution took place outside John Bowis's house in St Paul's Churchyard and by Topcliffe's arrangement the last words heard on earth by Father Pormort were the taunts and insults of his former convert.

46. *Joseph Lambton* seminary priest

Born at Malton, Yorkshire about May 1568
Hanged, drawn and quartered on Town Moor, Newcastle upon Tyne on 31 July, 1592, aged 24

JOSEPH LAMBTON was a member of the renowned Lambton family of Lambton, County Durham, and through his mother was a nephew of Father George Birkett, second Archpriest of England (1608-1614). Influenced by his uncle, Joseph was fifteen years of age when he crossed the seas to the English College at Rheims to begin his studies for the priesthood on 30 September 1584. He moved on to the Venerable English College in Rome on 18 August 1589, and was ordained priest in the Lateran Basilica on Holy Saturday, 28 March 1592.

In the early summer of 1592 Father Lambton set out for England, and his arrival in South Shields on the Tyne was eagerly awaited by his friends and also by his foes. There had been a breach of security in the Catholic organisation associated with Mrs Ursula Taylor's reception centre for priests and the civil authorities were aware that they were preparing to welcome two priests (Cashman, *Recusant History*, vol. X no. 4, p.231). Accordingly when Father Lambton's ship approached the quayside, the pursuivants were already in position and his Catholic friends could only watch from a distance. Fortunately the young priest was astute enough to recognise the danger, and managed to slip through the ranks of his unwelcome welcomers and make his own way to safety in Newcastle upon Tyne.

In this city, a few days later, the inexperienced priest took a walk in broad daylight along a public street and was recognised and arrested. His trial aroused much public interest. Never before had a member of the illustrious House of Lambton been charged as a common traitor. The common people were excited; the gentry attended in large numbers. The judges of the Assize were joined by Henry Hastings, the President of the Council of the North and by Toby Matthew the Dean of Durham. The Mayor and Corporation of Newcastle processed in solemn state to claim a place of honour. Amid all this ostentation the process of the law took its inevitable course. Father Lambton and his companion in the dock, Father Edward Waterson, were found guilty and sentenced to death.

The civic authorities were embarrassed by the disgrace they were inflicting on such a well known and highly respected family, and Mrs M.J. Cashman has noted how often Father Lambton's name has been suppressed in the official reports and documents of the time (*Recusant History*, vol. X no. 4, p.233). She suggests that 'the clerks did not care to record the fact that a Lambton had suffered the shameful penalty of high treason in a part of England where his name was such a great one'. The Catholics had no such inhibitions. They rejoiced and thanked God for another martyr who by his fidelity and courageous death had brought honour to himself and his family.

47. Anthony Page

seminary priest

Born at Harrow-on-the-Hill, Middlesex; date unknown
Hanged, drawn and quartered at York on 20 April, 1593

ANTHONY PAGE entered the English College at Rheims on 30 September 1584 and was ordained there on 21 September 1591. He set out for England on 3 January 1592, and served the Catholics of Yorkshire for a little over twelve months. The presence of Father Page at Mr John Hodgeson's house at Grosmont on the North Yorkshire Moors was reported by a Government spy, Thomas Clarke (Foley, *Records SJ*, VII 6), but the pursuivants missed the opportunity of capturing him.

Father Richard Holtby SJ, a Superior of the York mission, has written about 'the singular good zeal he (Father Page) had of souls, but especially towards the salvation of his worldly friends and kinsfolk', and refers to 'a long and dangerous journey taken into the south country' in an attempt to win these souls for Christ (*Troubles of our Catholic Forefathers*, III, 137-143).

On 2 February 1593 the Earl of Huntingdon, President of the Council of the North, ordered a sudden and intensive campaign throughout Yorkshire to catch as many Catholics as possible. The experienced priests immediately went underground and withdrew to places secret and safe. Father Page was not so fortunate. He took refuge at a Catholic house, Heworth Hall, then just outside the city of York, and when the house was raided (as the inhabitants knew it must be) the priest hid himself rather inexpertly under a haystack in an outhouse. It was an obvious place for a fugitive to hide and he was soon discovered and arrested.

Father Page was brought to trial at the Lenten Assizes in York and accused with him was the owner of Heworth Hall, Mr William Thwing, who had to face the charge of harbouring the priest and stood in some danger of sharing his death. The trial, however, was interrupted by Mr Thwing's sister, Anne, who proudly claimed full responsibility for welcoming Father Page to the family home at a time when her brother was absent. Mr Thwing was released but Anne Thwing was sent to prison and may have stayed there for the rest of her life.

Father Page was condemned to death for his priesthood but

remained so cheerful in prison and smiled so much that his captors complained that he was mocking them. He wrote many letters to prospective converts, and in a letter to his mother he told her he was going to die and that he intended to offer his life to God for her salvation. He never wavered in his faith, and when the time came he submitted himself bravely to the sufferings of a cruel death.

48. William Davies seminary priest

Born at Colwyn Bay, North Wales about 1555-1560
Hanged, drawn and quartered at Beaumaris, Anglesey on 27 July, 1593

WILLIAM DAVIES was admitted to the English College at Rheims on 6 April 1582, and was ordained priest on 5 April 1585. He set out for the Mission on 6 June 1585, and went immediately to his home district of North Wales, where for the next eight years he lived a very precarious life as a priest.

At first, Father Davies based himself with the dedicated Catholic layman, Mr Robert Pugh, at his isolated residence, Penrhyn Old Hall (now in the modern town of Llandudno), but in September 1586 the Earl of Pembroke, President of the Council of Wales, launched an intensive drive against the Catholics and the Old Hall had to be abandoned. Father Davies and his companions hid themselves in a cave in the Rhiwledyn cliffs on Little Orme's Head, and there, despite the Government prohibitions, they set up a printing press and produced Catholic books (*Biographical Studies*, II, p.37). The cave was raided by a local Justice of the Peace in April 1587 but the residents escaped safely.

Father Davies and Mr Pugh seem to have continued to work closely together until March 1592 when they were discovered by an ardent Protestant at Holyhead in Anglesey. Here they were endeavouring to make arrangements for four young men to travel to Ireland on the first stage of their journey to Spain, where they intended to enter the English College at Valladolid to study for the priesthood. In the confusion of the arrest Robert Pugh escaped, but

Father Davies and the four students were captured and taken to prison in Beaumaris Castle (Challoner, 1741, p.294-303, based on Diego de Yepes, 1599).

Father Davies was kept in solitary confinement for the next month but was then allowed to receive visitors, and such was his reputation for sanctity that Catholics flocked from all parts of the district to seek his advice and blessing and confess their sins.

All five prisoners were brought to trial in July 1592. Father Davies was accused of his priesthood; the others of helping him. All were found guilty and Father Davies at least should have been sentenced to death. The judges, however, were aware of the strength of feeling among the local people and the accusations of injustice that were being vehemently expressed by Catholics and non-Catholics alike; and, fearing the anger of the people, they refused to pass sentence and remanded the prisoners back to Beaumaris Castle.

Great efforts were then made by clergymen and Government officials to persuade Father Davies to renounce his faith and go free. He was sent to various conferences at Ludlow in Shropshire and then at Bewdley in Worcestershire, but he resolutely refused to accept their arguments and remained firm and constant in his allegiance. On 18 July 1593 a second trial took place in Beaumaris, and this time sentence was passed and Father Davies condemned to death. No local person was prepared to act as executioner for this well-loved priest, and the Sheriff was obliged to send to Chester, forty-two miles away, for a stranger to put into effect the decision of the Court.

The four students who had shared imprisonment with Father Davies were returned to prison and subsequently released. Two of them persevered in their vocations and were later ordained priests for the Mission (*Acts of the English Martyrs*, p.137).

49. *Edward Osbaldeston* seminary priest

Born at Osbaldeston, Blackburn in Lancashire in 1560
Hanged, drawn and quartered at York on 16 November, 1594, aged 34

EDWARD OSBALDESTON was a descendant of Thomas Stanley, the first Earl of Derby. He was a student at the English College at Rheims before January 1582, and was ordained priest on 21 September 1585. For some unexplained reason, he continued to live in Rheims for the next three and a half years and did not set out for the English Mission until 29 April 1589. For the next five years he worked in Yorkshire. In May 1593 a Government spy reported him as one 'who keep in Yorkshire but in what place I know not', (Foley, *Records SJ*, III, 6).

Father Osbaldeston was captured on 30 September 1594, while staying at an inn at Tollerton, about ten miles north-west of York. He has left his own written account of what happended and this is reprinted in volume III of Brother Henry Foley's *Records of the English Province of the Society of Jesus*. Father Osbaldeston was travelling in disguise and following the customary practice of the missionary priests was accompanied by a layman, Mr Francis Sayer of Worsall, Yarm. Together they posed as a merchant and his servant. In the Inn at Tollerton he recognised Thomas Clarke, a former priest and well known as a Government spy. He had the forlorn hope that he himself would not be recognised, but Thomas Clarke was not likely to miss an opportunity like this. He called the constable and during the night the priest was arrested.

Next day, Thomas Clarke conducted his captive to York and handed him over to the Council of the North, who lodged him in the house of Richard Outlaw, the pursuivant. Here he was closely examined but refused point blank to talk to those who wished to persuade him to give up his Faith.

Father Osbaldeston had a great desire to join the Society of Jesus and in his letters expressed a yearning to join the Catholic prisoners in York Castle where the seminary priests were living in community and practising their own form of religious life, but all this was denied to him. He was tried before the Council of the North and freely admitted his priesthood. He was sentenced to death and executed at the same time as several common criminals.

50. George Errington

layman

Born at Hirst, Woodhorn, Northumberland in 1554
Hanged, drawn and quartered at York on 29 November, 1596, aged 42

GEORGE ERRINGTON was educated at Trinity College, Oxford, and obtained his degree in 1579. Shortly afterwards he was reconciled to the Catholic Church and offered his services to Father Richard Holtby SJ, the superior of the Catholic mission in the north eastern counties. Father Holtby brought the layman into his underground movement and used him as a key figure in the secret and highly dangerous work of escorting newly-arrived priests from the port of South Shields to the safety of the mission headquarters at Grosmont on the North Yorkshire Moors.

Errington became a well trusted and highly successful courier in this most important work, and many priests were saved from disaster by his care and caution. In 1585, however, he was arrested on the quayside at Sandgate, a little down river from the centre of Newcastle, when he was about to embark on a French ship. He was accompanied by a young boy whom he was escorting to a continental seminary, which was a crime in the eyes of the Government. He was in further trouble when he was caught trying to smuggle nine secret letters out of the country (Catholic Record Society, vol. V, p.125).

George Errington was sent to London and kept in the Tower for over a year. He was released on bail of £100 on 3 February 1587, and at once returned to the north to continue his work for priests.

By this time his activities were well known to the authorities, and Henry Sanderson was commissioned by the Government 'to break the nest of that popish and traitorous crew' as Bishop Toby Matthew of Durham phrased it. The pursuit lasted until early in 1591, when Toby Matthew could report 'after long hunting from place to place to his great labour, cost and peril', Sanderson 'apprehended George Errington, hand to hand, being their chieftain and guide'. Errington was taken to York, made his appearance before Richard Topcliffe and the Council of the North on 22 May 1591, and was committed a prisoner to York Castle. He escaped almost immediately and returned to his work.

The response of the Government was to make his recapture a

pressing priority and he was, for a time, the most wanted recusant in the north. The intensive search succeeded and Errington's third and final arrest took place somewhere in County Durham in early November, 1593. He was returned to York Castle but was not brought to trial, and it would seem that the authorities were content to leave him in prison for the rest of his days. For three years he languished in idleness and was then caught in a trap set by one of his fellow prisoners, who pretended that he wished to become a Catholic and asked for help (Babthorpe, in *Troubles of our Catholic Forefathers* I, p.243). Errington responded to the invitation and was immediately denounced to the Council of the North for 'persuading to popery'. On this charge he was convicted, and he who had worked so closely with priests was himself executed like a priest by being hanged, drawn and quartered.

51. William Knight layman

Born at South Duffield, Howden, Yorkshire in 1573
Hanged, drawn and quartered at York on 29 November, 1596, aged 23

WILLIAM KNIGHT was only eighteen when he was first brought to court for his religion; but in the fine tradition of the Catholics of that time he failed to appear and the case was not pursued.

In 1593 the young man approached his uncle for possession of some land which his father had left in trust for him, but the uncle refused to hand over the land to a Catholic, and insisted that only by attending the state church could William Knight claim his inheritance. True to his faith, William refused to be blackmailed; and the uncle, to avoid further dispute, reported his nephew to the civil authorities and had him arrested as a Catholic (Grace Babthorpe's narration in *Troubles of our Catholic Forefathers*, p.245).

William Knight spent the rest of 1593 in prison in York Castle. On 8 January 1594 the Acts of the York High Commission record his removal to the custody of John Bestby and John Johnson, keepers of the Catholic prisoners within the Blockhouse at Kingston-upon-Hull, but by 1596 he was back in York Castle.

The Catholic prisoners formed a very close community and William Knight made many friends. Among them were George Errington and William Gibson, and two women, Mrs Ann Tesh and Mrs Bridget Maskew. It was to this group (as already related for George Errington) that a non-Catholic prisoner presented himself seeking advice as to how he could become a Catholic; they all gave him some assistance before discovering that it was a trap. They were all reported to the Council of the North and charged with the capital offence of 'persuading to popery'. They were found guilty and condemned to death.

The women were sentenced to be burned to death but reprieved by the Privy Council, who announced Her Majesty's pleasure that the executions should be delayed until further instructions were given. In fact they were kept in prison for seven years until, at the accession of King James I, they secured their release.

William Knight was condemned to be hanged, drawn and quartered, and he was executed at the same time as George Errington and William Gibson.

52. William Gibson layman

Born near Ripon; date unknown
Hanged, drawn and quartered at York on 29 November, 1596

THE ACT BOOKS of the Court of High Commission at York provide the only known official reference to the life of William Gibson. There he is mentioned as a servant of Mrs Elizabeth Thynne. Both were called by the Commissioners in 1581 to explain their absence from the Anglican Church services, and both refused to give any undertaking that they would attend in the future. They were accordingly committed to prison, and it is possible that William Gibson stayed in prison for the remaining fifteen years of his life. Certainly in 1626, when the reminiscences of Mrs Elizabeth Ellison of Cliffe, East Yorkshire, were published in the Chalcedon Returns, she remembered William Gibson as a man who 'was many years a prisoner in York Castle for his religion'.

J.C.H. Aveling (*Northern Catholics*, p.187) has established that Mrs Elizabeth Thynne lived at Brafferton in the old wapentake of Bulmer, a few miles north of York, and this would be where William Gibson lived and worked, at least for a time.

He was another victim of the trick that was played on a group of Catholic prisoners in York Castle by the bogus convert in 1596. With the others he was accused of 'persuading to popery', and with George Errington and William Knight he was hanged, drawn and quartered.

53. Christopher Robinson seminary priest

Born at Woodside, Carlisle, Cumberland about 1565-1570
Hanged, drawn and quartered at Carlisle about March 1597

CHRISTOPHER ROBINSON arrived at the English College at Rheims on 17 April 1589, and was ordained priest by Cardinal Philip Sega in Rheims on 24 February 1592. He set out for the English Mission on 1 September 1592, and for the next five years worked as a priest in his home district of Westmorland and Cumberland.

He made a special journey to Durham in 1594 to witness the trial and martyrdom of his Westmorland friend, St John Boste, and wrote a vivid account of these events and his own reaction to them in a long letter to another Westmorland friend, Father Richard Dudley (Catholic Record Society vol. 1, pp.85-92).

Father Robinson was captured on 4 March 1597, through the machinations of Thomas Lancaster, a professional priest-catcher in the employ of the Bishop of Carlisle. The arrest took place at the home of Mr Leonard Musgrave and his wife Margaret, at Johnby Hall, about six miles from Penrith (Bamber, in *Recusant History*, IV, 30). The priest and his hosts were taken to prison in Carlisle, and later the Musgraves were granted a royal pardon. Father Robinson was brought to trial and condemned to death.

In prison, he was visited by one of his Protestant relatives, Henry Robinson, then Provost of Queen's College, Oxford, and later Bishop of Carlisle. This distinguished visitor made repeated efforts, by praise and promises rather than by threats and fear, to persuade the prisoner to conform to the State Church, but his efforts were totally unsuccessful.

Father Leo Bamber, using the 1597 letter of Father Henry Garnett SJ, has described the execution of Father Christopher Robinson. As they tried to hang him the rope broke twice and the condemned man remonstrated with the Sheriff, saying that although he was perfectly willing to die, these long delays in the process of death showed little humanity. They then fastened two ropes together for their third attempt and the martyr said, 'By this means I shall be longer a-dieing: but it is no matter, I am willing to suffer all'.

54. *John Bretton* layman

Born at West Bretton, Sandal Magna, West Yorkshire, about 1529
Hanged at York on 1 April, 1598, aged about 69

JOHN BRETTON was a married man with five children and owned about 180 acres of land at West Bretton and near Dewsbury. He has been described by Father Hugh Bowler OSB as 'a gentleman farmer of moderate means' (*Biographical Studies* II, pp.111-134).

In October 1577, when Edwin Sandys, Archbishop of York submitted a list of Yorkshire Catholics to the Privy Council, he included the names of John and Frances Bretton and described them as 'most obstinate and perverse'. For safety's sake, John took flight and remained in hiding for the next sixteen years. His presence was demanded at the Manorial Court of the Rectory Manor of Dewsbury in October, 1580, and the Court threatened to seize his lands because he had not appeared before them for six years or more, but no John Bretton appeared. During this prolonged absence, John's non-Catholic brother, Robert Bretton, acted as steward of the Bretton lands, and between August 1582 and March 1584 Robert was summoned eight times before the High Commission in York and ordered to produce his brother in person. Each time he failed.

John Bretton did make a fleeting appearance at Salford in Lancashire, where he was in prison as a recusant from 3 September until 27 December 1585, but the details are obscure and serve only to indicate the probable area in which he was hiding. In April 1586, the Manorial Court at Dewsbury carried out its previous threat and actually seized the Bretton lands. On this occasion John did appear and appealed successfully against the decision. He then withdrew again to his hiding place.

In 1593, when a new Penal Law against the Catholics ordered all recusants to return to their homes or suffer the loss of all their property, John Bretton at last returned to his estate. He lived quietly and for his recusancy was fined five times in the next two years. Needless to say, there is no record that he ever paid these fines, and he continued to show his disregard for all the implications of the Penal Laws until early in 1598 when he was arrested.

John Bretton was brought to trial at the York Assizes on 31 March 1598, and charged with using seditious words against the Queen's Majesty. It was commonly believed by the Catholics of his time that his 'seditious words' consisted merely of the pious hope that a Catholic monarch would soon succeed the now ageing Queen, but a different interpretation was placed on his words by the Court and his past record cannot have helped his case. He was found guilty, sentenced to death and hanged.

55. *Peter Snow* seminary priest

Born near Ripon, Yorkshire; date unknown
Hanged, drawn and quartered at York on 15 June, 1598

PETER SNOW entered the English College at Rheims on 17 April, 1589, and was ordained priest at Soissons on 31 March 1591. He left the College for England on 15 May 1591, and worked on the Yorkshire mission for seven years. He was one of the priests seen at

John Hodgeson's house at Grosmont, North Yorkshire, in 1593 by the spy Thomas Clarke, but his other missionary activities seem to have escaped the record.

Father Snow was captured with his lay companion Mr Ralph Grimston as they were on the road going towards York (Challoner, 1741, Part 1, p.360). Both were brought to trial before the Council of the North in York, and Father Snow was found guilty of treason because he was a priest. The fact of his death as a martyr is well established from the Catalogues of Martyrs.

56. *Ralph Grimston* layman

Born probably at Nidd Hall, near Knaresborough, West Yorkshire; date unknown
Hanged at York on 15 June, 1598

RALPH GRIMSTON was a gentleman living at Nidd Hall and seems to have been a devoted Catholic all his life. He was married and two or three of his sons were overseas at seminaries. He was well known to the authorities as a leading recusant, and Nidd Hall was often used as a place of refuge for priests and a meeting place where Catholics gathered for Mass.

In November 1593, Ralph Grimston was arrested and questioned by the Council of the North in York. (Foley, *Records SJ*, III, p.760). He was committed to prison in York Castle but was later released. Even while he was in prison Nidd Hall continued to be used as a meeting place for Catholics, and Ralph Fisher, a layman who later became a seminary priest, was arrested there and charged with non-attendance at the services of the Established Church.

On 1 May 1598 Ralph Grimston was conducting Father Peter Snow towards York when both were arrested on the open road. The layman tried to defend his priest by 'lifting up his weapon' but his gesture was of no avail and they were taken to York to be tried by the Council of the North. Father Snow was condemned and executed as a priest and Mr Grimston was condemned and executed for harbouring him.

57. *Christopher Wharton* seminary priest

Born at Middleton, Ilkley, Yorkshire in 1540
Hanged, drawn and quartered at York on 28 March, 1600, aged 60

CHRISTOPHER WHARTON became a member of Trinity College, Oxford, in 1559, was elected a Fellow in June 1563 and proceeded MA in February 1565. Subsequently he was converted to Catholicism and was over forty years of age when he entered the English College at Rheims on 28 July 1583 to prepare himself for the priesthood. He was ordained priest by Cardinal Louis de Guise on 31 March 1584, and remained at his studies for another two years before setting out for the English Mission on 21 May 1586.

For the next thirteen years Father Wharton worked as a priest in his native Yorkshire. In 1599 he was staying at the house of Mrs Eleanor Hunt in the grounds of Sir William Ingleby's Ripley Castle when he fell foul of the notorious priest hunter Sir William Procter of Fountain's Abbey, and both priest and hostess were arrested.

Imprisoned in York Castle, they were among the fifty-three Catholic prisoners who were assembled by force each week to listen to a Protestant sermon. Father William Richmond has described in *True Story of the Catholic Prisoners in York Castle* how Father Wharton, when compelled to attend a sermon by the Archbishop of York, rose with an old Marian priest, Father George Rains, to make formal protest with courage and courtesy.

At the Lenten Assizes in York in 1600 Father Wharton was brought to trial. He was accused of being a priest and freely admitted that he was, but knowing the relevant Statute of 1585 very well, he pointed out that its provisions applied only to such priests as were ordained after 1559. He challenged the court to prove that he himself had been ordained after that date. It was unfortunate that one of the judges, John Savile, had been at Oxford with Father Wharton in the 1560s and could state categorically that at that time Christopher Wharton was a layman and therefore must have been ordained later than 1559. The evidence was conclusive in law, and Father Wharton was convicted and executed on the Friday of Easter Week, 1600. Mrs Eleanor Hunt, accused of harbouring the priest, was also found guilty and sentenced to death; but she was reprieved, and seems to have spent the rest of her life in prison.

58. *Thomas Sprott* seminary priest

Born at Skelsmergh, Kendal, Westmorland in 1571
Hanged, drawn and quartered in Lincoln on 1 July, 1600, aged 29

THOMAS SPROTT was ordained at the English College, Douai in 1596 and set out in May for England. While travelling through Holland he was arrested at the town of Brielle, which was then an English possession, and he completed his journey to London as a prisoner. He spent about six months in the Bridewell prison in London before making his escape with nine other Catholic prisoners. He was given food and lodging by the Jesuit Superior, Father Henry Garnett, and then guided to a safer part of the country (Garnett's letters in Grene's Collection P).

Father Sprott was one of the many English priests who signed the letter of 8 November 1598 to Pope Clement VIII in which they affirmed their loyalty to the Holy See and welcomed the appointment of the first Archpriest for the English Mission, Father George Blackwell.

After about three years of ministry Father Sprott was staying with Father Thomas Hunt at the Saracen's Head Inn in Lincoln when a disturbance took place as a mob hunted some highwaymen. In the confusion of the chase all strangers were suspect and the two priests were questioned. To clear themselves they said they were Catholics who had left home to escape the effects of the Penal Laws, but this explanation only served to suggest to the mob that they might be priests. They were searched, and rosary beads, holy oils and breviaries were discovered on their persons. They were formally arrested and brought to trial at the Assizes (Verstegan's account, 1601).

The trial began in great confusion as the priests were accused of a wide variety of Catholic offences but then all charges were reduced to the one that they were Catholic priests. No witnesses were called and no evidence was produced. The judge, Sir John Glanville, simply insisted that the prisoners should admit that they were priests. This they refused to do and angered the judge so much with their determination that he lost his temper and instructed the jury to bring in an immediate verdict of guilty.

Sentenced to death in these circumstances, the priests excited some compassion among those who attended their execution. From the scaffold they both proclaimed that they were dying not for treason but for the Catholic religion, and both died bravely for their Faith.

59. *Thomas Hunt* seminary priest

Born in Norfolk in 1574
Hanged, drawn and quartered at Lincoln on 1 July, 1600, aged 26

THOMAS HUNT'S real name was Thomas Benstead, and he was admitted to the English College at Valladolid on 12 May 1592. According to the College Register, he was nineteen years of age. He stayed for about eight months and was then transferred to another Spanish college, the newly opened English College at Seville. After six years of preparation he was ordained priest in April 1599, and set out on the hazardous journey across Europe from the south of Spain through France to his mission in England.

On arriving in London Father Hunt was helped by Father Henry Garnett SJ, but seems to have uttered some careless words which were betrayed to the authorities and, as Father Robert Persons SJ has reported, he was by December 1599 a prisoner in the Clink. From there he was moved to the special prison for priests at Wisbech Castle in Cambridgeshire, and on 17 March 1600 Father Anthony Rivers SJ could give the news in one of his letters that Hunt, alias Benstead, was one of the six priests who had recently escaped.

Again Father Hunt was helped by Father Henry Garnett SJ in London before beginning a new missionary apostolate in Lincolnshire. In April 1600 he celebrated the first anniversary of his ordination to the priesthood, and two months later his final arrest took place when he met Father Thomas Sprott at the Saracen's Head in the city of Lincoln. Father Hunt's trial and martyrdom have already been described in the account of Father Thomas Sprott.

60. *Robert Nutter* Dominican priest

Born at Burnley, Lancashire about 1557
Hanged, drawn and quartered at Lancaster on 26 July, 1600, aged about 43

ROBERT NUTTER arrived with his older brother John at the English College at Rheims towards the end of August 1579. Robert was ordained priest at Soissons on 22 December 1581 and set out for the English Mission on 4 January 1582. For two years he was a highly successful travelling priest. His worth was recognised not only by the Catholic communities he visited in Oxfordshire, Berkshire, Buckinghamshire, Hampshire, Sussex and London, but also by the Government agents, one of whom, Thomas Dodwell, named him as one of the six priests in England who ought to 'be apprehended with as much speed as may be' (Foley, *Records*, VI, 719).

In 1584 Father Nutter was captured in Oxford, and at the beginning of February was in the Tower of London. The Tower Diary for 1584 shows that the prisoner was loaded with chains, tortured by that evil contraption, the Scavenger's daughter, and subjected to all the horrors of the dungeon known as the pit. In addition to all these physical pains, Father Robert Nutter suffered the anguish of knowing that his brother, Father John Nutter, was also a prisoner somewhere in the Tower and would soon be taken to his martyrdom at Tyburn.

After twelve months' confinement in these conditions Father Robert Nutter was suddenly released, and, on 21 January 1585, was one of the twenty priests deported from the country and forbidden to return under pain of death. He made his way to the English College at Rheims and it is clear from the Douai Diary that by July he was already engaged in the highly dangerous work of smuggling young men out of England to the continental seminaries. For Father Nutter this involved many journeys backwards and forwards across the English Channel and in November he was captured on a French ship off the coast of Kent and taken to Newgate prison in London (Catholic Record Society, vol. V, p.155).

Father Nutter spent the next fifteen years in prison. For most of this time he was in the special prison for priests at Wisbech Castle in Cambridgeshire where he endured all the difficulties of that embarrassing quarrel that is known as the Wisbech Stirs and found himself an unwilling participant in the controversies over the appointment of England's first Archpriest. It was while he was in prison at Wisbech that Father Nutter recognised his Dominican vocation and by adroitly smuggling letters past the gaolers he obtained permission from the Spanish Provincial of the Order to make his religious profession as a friar.

On 10 March 1600, Father Nutter and five other priests escaped from Wisbech. Three of the party moved southwards towards London and were soon re-captured but the others sought safety in the north and Father Nutter was soon back in his native Lancashire. He joined Father Edward Thwing in his apostolate and for two months he ministered again to the people he had come to serve. Then, early in May, both priests were arrested as they returned from a visit to Father Richard Cowling SJ.

Father Nutter was taken to Lancaster Castle and tried at the Lancaster Summer Assizes in July. He was condemned to death for his priesthood, and Bishop Challoner has quoted Dr Champney's tribute that 'he went to the gallows with as much cheerfulness and joy as if he had been going to a feast' (Challoner, 1741, Part 1, p.384).

61. Edward Thwing seminary priest

Born at Heworth, York, in 1565
Hanged, drawn and quartered at Lancaster on 26 July, 1600, aged 35

EDWARD THWING entered the English College at Rheims on 22 July 1583, but his health was not good and he was obliged to seek medical treatment away from the College. On 20 July 1585 he resumed his studies for the priesthood, and in November 1587 moved on to the Venerable English College in Rome. Again his health troubled him and he had to return to the more suitable northern climate of Rheims. He was ordained priest at Laon on 20 December 1590.

Father Thwing was not considered to be strong enough for the hardships of the English mission and was therefore appointed to a teaching position in the seminary. For seven years his pursuits were academic but in 1597 he was allowed to fulfill his real ambition and return to England to begin his missionary apostolate.

At first he worked alone on the Lancashire mission but in late March 1600 he was joined by Father Robert Nutter who had just escaped from Wisbech Castle. The partnership was not destined to last long. Within two months both priests were captured and in prison in Lancaster Castle. They were interrogated by Thomas Hesketh who reported to Sir Robert Cecil that 'Thwing had been a scholar of some understanding and much esteemed among the papists'. On 4 July Father Thwing demonstrated his theological capabilities by taking the leading part in a public disputation with the Vicar of Kendal and the Vicar of Lancaster.

From his prison, he wrote many letters to his friends and family, and Dr Thomas Worthington, President of Douai, has preserved two of these letters addressed to himself. In the first, Father Thwing describes himself as 'a prisoner for Christ in Lancaster Castle expecting nothing but execution at the next Assizes'. and he signs the letter 'from my prison paradise'. In the second letter he writes 'I shall if God make me worthy conclude an unhappy life with a most happy death'. (Challoner, 1741, Part I, p.381).

Father Thwing had prepared well for his martyr's death with Father Robert Nutter and both priests edified the large number of Catholics who were present in the watching crowd.

62. *Thomas Palaser* seminary priest

Born at Kirby Wiske, Yorkshire, about 1570
Hanged, drawn and quartered at Durham on 8 September, 1600, aged about 30

THOMAS PALASER arrived at the English College at Rheims on 24 July 1592, and then moved on to the English College at Valladolid in Spain where he was admitted on 3 January 1593. He was ordained priest by the Archbishop of Burgos and towards the end of 1596 returned from a Spain hostile to Englishmen to an England hostile to Catholics.

He was captured almost as soon as he arrived in London, and certainly by 18 March 1597 was a prisoner in the Gatehouse. As a loyal Englishman he did not hesitate to make use of his Spanish experiences and provided the Government with much military information about the Spanish preparations for their projected invasion of England (Letter to the Privy Council, 18 March 1597). His services as a spy did not, however, procure his release from prison, and hearing that Topcliffe the torturer was about to visit him, Father Palaser took matters into his own hands and made his escape.

For the next three years, Father Palaser worked as an active missionary priest in the area of Durham and North Yorkshire. J.C.H. Aveling has picked up traces of his presence at Worsall, Northallerton, Osmotherley, Lartington and South Otterington (*Northern Catholics*, p.152).

On 24 June 1600 Father Palaser was at the house of Mr and Mrs John Norton at Ravensworth near Gateshead in County Durham when the establishment was raided by the Government agent, Henry Sanderson, and all present were arrested. In reporting the matter to the Privy Council, Toby Matthew, the Bishop of Durham, called Father Palaser 'a lusty bold fellow' and adds that 'superstitious massing stuff and prohibited books' were found in the house.

Father Palaser and his friends were brought to trial at Durham and, with Mr John Norton and Mr John Talbot, he was found guilty and put to death. Father Thomas Fitzherbert wrote in 1602 that he was condemned 'only for being a priest'.

63. *John Norton* layman

Born probably at Norton Conyers, North Yorkshire; date unknown
Hanged at Durham on 8 September, 1600

IT WAS in John Norton's house at Ravensworth near Gateshead, County Durham, that Thomas Palaser (above) was captured on 24 June 1600, and John and his wife Margaret were arrested with the priest. John Norton belonged to the old Catholic family of Norton Conyers in the North Riding, and was related to the Richard Norton who had taken part in the Pilgrimage of Grace and the six Nortons who suffered as a result of their participation in the Earls' Rising of 1569. John himself, however, does not appear to have always been a Catholic. Miss A.C.M. Forster has suggested (*Recusant History*, vol. 6 no. 2), that the reason for Father Palaser's visit to the Norton home at Ravensworth was to reconcile the whole family to the Catholic Church.

John Norton may not have been a Catholic very long but he reacted with the traditional vehemence of his family when his house was raided to capture a priest. He seized a gun and fired it several times before he was held at the point of a rapier.

Taken to prison in Durham, John Norton and his wife were brought to trial and sentenced to death at the same time as Father Palaser and Mr John Talbot; but as Mrs Margaret Norton was with child she was reprieved, and on 5 December 1601 granted a Royal Pardon. It is the wording of this Pardon which establishes her offence, and therefore that of the others, as being a contravention of the Statute of 1585 which made any assistance given to a priest a capital offence.

When Father Thomas Palaser was hanged, drawn and quartered at Durham, his protectors Mr John Norton and Mr John Talbot were hanged as well.

64. John Talbot layman

Born at Thornton-le-Street, North Yorkshire in 1562
Hanged at Durham on 8 September, 1600, aged 38

JOHN TALBOT was a persistent recusant all his life. In his study of the Talbot family (*Recusant History* vol. 2, no. 1, pp.4-22), Father Hugh Bowler OSB has noted that John's name is missing from the official family pedigrees of the Visitations of 1612 and 1666 and suggests that these may be the deliberate omissions of a recusant from Government records. He then uses the Exchequer Records to produce a life story of John Talbot from his first fine for recusancy on 18 March, 1587, to his final conviction on 2 April 1599, for refusing to attend the services of the Anglican Church.

On 24 June 1600 John Talbot was in Mr John Norton's house at Ravensworth in County Durham when Father Thomas Palaser was arrested, and as Mr Norton reached for his gun, Mr Talbot drew his sword (Leonard Brackenbury's evidence in the *Chalcedon Returns* of 1622). In prison in Durham he was offered his life if he would conform to the Established Church. For a life-long recusant there could only be one answer to that offer, and John Talbot's life of fidelity to his Faith was ended when he was hanged at Durham in 1600.

65. Roger Filcock Jesuit priest

Born at Sandwich, Kent, about 1570
Hanged, drawn and quartered at Tyburn, London on 27 February, 1601, aged about 31

ROGER FILCOCK entered the English College at Rheims on 15 June 1588, and was sent on 29 September 1590 to the English College at Valladolid, where he was ordained priest. He began the hazardous journey back to England in October 1597, and travelled by sea from Bilbao. On 13 December 1597, at the French port of Calais, he and his companions had a narrow escape from being captured by the Dutch. Probably early in 1598, Father Filcock began his work on the English mission.

Father Henry Garnett SJ, the Jesuit Superior, reported in a letter of 1601 that he had admitted Father Filcock into the Society of Jesus (Foley, *Records SJ*, VII, p.1359), and Charles Dodd, the eminent Catholic historian, was taken very much to task in 1741 by Father John Constable SJ because he had failed to mention this fact in his Church History.

On 7 July 1600, Father Garnett reported in another letter that Father Filcock had been captured and that he had been betrayed by John Ingleby, a former student of the English College, Valladolid (Catholic Record Society, vol. XXX, p.35). Father Filcock was lodged in Newgate prison until his trial at the London Sessions on 26 February 1601. In court he refused to be tried by a jury, because, as he said in his own written account, he did not wish these poor men to be guilty of his innocent blood. It was therefore the Recorder himself, John Croke, who pronounced the priest guilty and sentenced him to death.

Next day, in company with Blessed Mark Barkworth OSB, Father Filcock was dragged on a hurdle from Newgate to Tyburn. The procession arrived at the gallows sooner than expected and the priests had to wait while St Anne Line and a number of thieves were being hanged. When Father Filcock's turn came, he proudly confessed that he was a Catholic priest and a Jesuit and stated clearly that he died for his faith and his priesthood. (Foley, *Records SJ*, VII p.1359)

66. Robert Middleton

Jesuit priest

Born at York in 1570
Hanged, drawn and quartered at Lancaster on 3 April, 1601, aged 31

ROBERT MIDDLETON studied at the English College at Douai from 1594 until 1597 and then entered the Venerable English College in Rome on 14 April 1597. He was ordained priest on 4 January 1598, and left Rome for England on 20 April 1598. He spent less than two years on the Yorkshire mission and was captured at Christmastime 1599 in a house at Ripon and taken to prison in York. He promptly escaped but for safety's sake crossed the Pennines to continue his apostolate in Lancashire.

On 30 September 1600 he was caught again. This time it happened on the highway at the Fylde near Preston and he was taken to prison in Preston where under interrogation he gave an account of his life to the Justice of the Peace, Sir Richard Houghton. Father Middleton was taken by his captors from Preston to Lancaster and on the way a group of well-intentioned Catholics under the leadership of Father Thurstan Hunt made an heroic but ill-judged attempt to rescue him. It was an affair of violence: stones were thrown, swords used and a gun fired, but all was in vain. Father Middleton was not rescued, and he was now joined in captivity by Father Hunt.

The priests were taken to prison in Lancaster and the provoked authorities treated them harshly. The Privy Council was alarmed and summoned them both to London for more questioning. All in all, the rescue attempt had only served to increase the bitterness of the persecution. While in prison in the Gatehouse in London, Father Middleton made his profession as a Jesuit and was accepted into the Society by Father Henry Garnett (Foley, *Records SJ*, vol. VII, p.963).

Father Middleton and Father Hunt were returned to Lancaster to stand trial at the Lenten Assizes. They were condemned to death for being priests and on the scaffold they wore their priestly cassocks with pride and sought each other's blessing before they died. Then they were hanged, drawn and quartered.

67. Thurstan Hunt seminary priest

Born at Carlton Hall, Rothwell, near Leeds, Yorkshire in 1555
Hanged, drawn and quartered at Lancaster on 3 April, 1601, aged 46

THURSTAN HUNT, also known as Robert Greenlow, arrived at the English College at Rheims on 18 September 1583, and was ordained priest on 20 April 1585. He returned to England later that year and landed at Sandwich in Kent. From there he made his way northwards and for the next fifteen years worked as a priest in Lancashire, Yorkshire and Cheshire.

On 30 September 1601 Father Hunt was the leader of the Catholic attempt to rescue Father Middleton from custody and during the fracas he used his gun to defend himself. It was all in vain; Father Middleton was not rescued, and Father Hunt joined him in captivity. The audacity of this attack and the use of violence seriously alarmed the Government and invited reprisals. In prison in Preston both priests suffered the repercussions and when the Mayor of Preston searched Father Hunt he found on his person three dangerous letters. Two were from the Archpriest, Father George Blackwell, and gave valuable information about Catholic affairs. The third was the draft of an open letter from Father Hunt to Queen Elizabeth warning her of an alleged Puritan plot to replace her on the throne by the Earl of Essex.

The Privy Council took all these matters very seriously, but the members were more concerned about the implications of the rescue attempt than about any allegations of a plot. Father Hunt and Father Middleton were taken to London for further questioning, and from his prison in the capital Father Hunt wrote an open declaration in which he re-affirmed his belief in the reality of the plot and expressed his hope for some gesture of kindness from the Government in return for his warning. The response of the Government was to return him to Preston for trial, and he and Father Middleton were executed together as priests on 3 April 1601.

68. *John Sugar* seminary priest

Born at Wombourne, near Wolverhampton, Staffordshire in 1558
Hanged, drawn and quartered at Warwick on 16 July, 1604, aged 46

JOHN SUGAR was a lay minister or reader in the Church of England when he entered St Mary's Hall, Oxford, on 30 October 1584. He left University without a degree and became the Vicar of Cannock in Staffordshire. Some time after this he was converted to Catholicism and presented himself at the English College at Douai on 25 June 1599. He was ordained priest on 21 April 1601, and set out for England on 4 October of that year. Bishop Richard Challoner uses 'an old manuscript now lost' to establish that Father Sugar worked as a priest in the Midlands and 'travelled afoot very much' in Warwickshire, Staffordshire and Worcestershire.

Father Sugar was staying with Mr Robert Grissold at Rowington in Warwickshire on 8 July 1603, when they were surprised by the arrival of the pursuivants. The priest made his escape but was captured on the open road and with Mr Grissold was taken to prison in Warwick. At Warwick Assizes, Father Sugar was found guilty of being a priest; but sentence was delayed while representations for a Royal Pardon were made to the new King James I, who was said to be reluctant to persecute his Catholic subjects. During this interlude, which lasted twelve months, Father Sugar was subjected to great pressure from the local authorities to give up his faith, but he resisted all persuasions.

The special pardon requested never arrived, and at Warwick Assizes on 13 July 1604 Father Sugar was sentenced to death. On his final morning, according to Bishop Challoner, he told his friends to be merry 'for we have occasion not for sorrow but joy', and on the scaffold he announced clearly that he died for his Faith and was in no way guilty of treason.

69. Robert Grissold layman

Born at Rowington, Warwickshire between 1550 and 1560
Hanged at Warwick on 16 July, 1604

THE GRISSOLDS were a well known Catholic family and the name appears very frequently in the Recusant Rolls. Robert Grissold in particular was fined £80 in 1593 and £60 in 1594 for not attending the services of the Church of England. On 8 July 1603, when the Grissold house was raided by the pursuivants, Robert helped Father Sugar to escape and with him was arrested on the highway. In Warwick prison, the layman showed his respect and love for the priest by refusing the opportunity of making his escape unless Father Sugar could escape with him.

Robert Grissold was a simple agricultural worker with little education but he resisted all attempts to persuade him to give up his religion and never wavered in his faith. In Court, during his trial, one of the Justices shouted at him in exasperation, 'Grissold, Grissold, go to church or else thou shalt be hanged'. On the scaffold he said that he died 'not for theft nor for felony but for conscience'. Without flinching he watched the cruelties inflicted on Father Sugar and then calmly offered himself to the hangman.

70. Robert Drury seminary priest

Born in Buckinghamshire in 1568
Hanged, drawn and quartered at Tyburn on 26 February, 1607, aged 39

ROBERT DRURY was a student at the English College at Rheims on 1 April 1588, and was sent to the newly founded English College at Valladolid where his entry is recorded for 24 October 1590. He was ordained priest by the Bishop of Leon in 1595 and returned to England that same year.

For the next twelve years Father Drury worked as a priest in the London area. He was convinced that the progress of the Church in England demanded the presence of a Bishop, and when, in 1598,

Father George Blackwell was appointed Archpriest of the Mission, he expressed his disappointment by joining a group of priests called the Appellants and writing to Rome in protest. As a result of this letter Father Drury was suspended by the Archpriest, and although he offered his submission immediately, he was not exonerated until 5 October 1602, when a papal brief declared that the suspension had been invalid.

In January 1603 Father Drury was one of thirteen priests who signed an address of loyalty to Queen Elizabeth. The acknowledged her as their lawful Queen while reserving the right to accept the spiritual authority of the Pope. This address of loyalty was not very popular among the English Catholics, and was largely ineffectual as the Queen was close to death and did in fact die on 24 March 1603.

Father Drury was arrested on 10 February 1607 at Mr John Stanesby's house near the present Whitefriars Street in London. His indictment has been preserved and is printed in the Catholic Record Society's volume XXIV (p.24). This shows that he was accused of violating the Act of 1585 by being ordained priest overseas and then coming into England. At the Newgate Sessions he and Father William Davies were found guilty of treason, but before sentence was passed they were offered the King's mercy if they would take the Oath of Allegiance which had been introduced in June 1606. For some time they considered this and were uncertain what to do. In fact this Oath had already been condemned by the Holy See and as soon as this information reached them, they refused it immediately.

Brought back to Court for sentencing on 25 February 1607, the judges gave them a formal choice: take the oath or be sentenced to death. Both priests chose death. Father Davies was later reprieved by King James I at the request of the French Ambassador, but there was no reprieve for Father Drury.

In company with an assorted collection of thirty-two thieves and murderers he was taken from Newgate prison to Tyburn. The criminals rode in a cart; the priest was dragged on a hurdle. On the scaffold, the Sheriff offered the Oath of Allegiance again, but Father Drury was quite resolute and accepted death as a loyal son of the Church.

71. *Matthew Flathers* seminary priest

Born at Weston, near Otley, West Yorkshire in 1560
Hanged, drawn and quartered at York on 21 March, 1608, aged 48

MAIOR FLATHERS matriculated at University College, Oxford, on 2 July 1585 and obtained his degree on 27 February 1590. Some time after this he became a Catholic and was over forty years of age when he entered the English College at Douai on 18 August 1604. He changed his name from 'Maior' to the christian name of 'Matthew' on the occasion of his Confirmation on 22 March 1605. He was ordained priest at Arras on 25 March 1606, and set out for the English mission on 30 June that same year.

Father Flathers arrived in England just a few days after the public announcement of the Royal Proclamation which banished all priests from the country, and so his first stay in England as a priest was very brief. Within a matter of days he was on the return journey to Douai but like many of the deported priests he merely paused in the English College before taking the next available ship back to England.

On his second expedition, Father Flathers preserved his freedom only a little longer than on his first. In August 1607 he was with Father William Mush and Father Cuthbert Trollope at Upsall Castle, South Kilvington, near Thirsk in Yorkshire, when that persistent priest hunter, Sir Stephen Procter of Fountain's Abbey, attacked the castle. Father Trollope escaped but Father Flathers and Father William Mush were captured and with 'the gentlewoman who was caring for them', (probably Lady Constable, the widow of Sir Henry) they were taken to prison in York.

All were brought to trial at the Lent Assizes in York in 1608. The priests were accused of their priesthood; the lady of harbouring them. All were found guilty and sentenced to death and all refused to take the Oath of Allegiance which could have saved them from the gallows.

In fact, the lady was reprieved and sent to prison indefinitely. Father William Mush escaped. Father Flathers remained to die alone. The Third Douai Diary says that 'he was sentenced to death because he was a priest but then executed because he refused to take the Oath'.

72. Roger Cadwallador seminary priest

Born at Stretton Sugwas in Herefordshire in 1566
Hanged, drawn and quartered at Leominster, Herefordshire on 27 August, 1610, aged 44

ROGER CADWALLADOR arrived at the English College at Rheims on 26 March 1590, and when he moved to the English College at Valladolid in January 1593 he was already a deacon. He was ordained priest by the Bishop of Zamora and set out for England in the same year of 1593.

For the remaining sixteen years of his life Father Cadwallador worked as a travelling priest in and around Herefordshire. He was one of the Appellants who signed the formal appeal against the Archpriest, Father George Blackwell, on 17 November 1600, and he was one of thirteen priests who offered a protestation of loyalty to Queen Elizabeth in 1603.

In 1605 there was much unrest among the Catholics of Herefordshire as they came to realise that the promises of King James I about religious toleration were not likely to be fulfilled. The Earl of Worcester was sent to the area in a show of force to prevent disturbances and the activities of Father Cadwallador came under close scrutiny. He was accused of treason and for a short time had to flee or go into hiding. A list of people said to have attended Mass at Whitfield near Hereford names Father Cadwallador as 'the priest who usually said Mass there'.

Father Cadwallador was captured near Hereford on 8 April 1610. He was questioned by Robert Bennett, the Bishop of Hereford, who offered him the opportunity to take the Oath of Allegiance and go free; but the priest, with great determination, refused.

He suffered much from his experience of the harsh prison conditions of the time and was very ill when the time for his trial approached. The Herefordshire Assizes that year were held fourteen miles away in Leominster because the plague was raging in Hereford. The enfeebled priest, shackled and carrying his heavy chains, was forced to walk the whole distance. He was found guilty of his priesthood and condemned to death.

On the day of his execution, he was twice offered his life if he would take the Oath but he persisted in his refusal. On the gallows he told the spectators that he was being put to death for his priesthood and not for any other reason. The hostile crowd grew very sympathetic as unskilful executioners prolonged the priest's agony and they heckled the ineptitude that was causing so much extra torment to a helpless victim. In such circumstances Father Cadwallador died with amazing fortitude and his death had a profound effect on all who saw him die.

73. Thomas Atkinson seminary priest

Born in Yorkshire about 1545
Hanged, drawn and quartered in York on 11 March, 1616, aged 70

THOMAS ATKINSON was about forty years of age when he arrived at the English College at Rheims probably in 1585. He was ordained priest at Laon on 11 June 1588, and departed for England on the following 11 November. He worked on the Yorkshire mission and at first formed a partnership with an experienced local priest, Blessed William Andleby. Professor John Bossy has described how 'Anlaby started in 1578, tramping with his kit in a bag, then bought a horse and joined up with Atkinson, with whom he served an extensive territory running from Richmond to Hull. Anlaby was arrested in 1597, and so apparently was the horse, for Atkinson thereafter went the round on foot' (*English Catholic Community*, p.253).

Lady Grace Babthorpe of Osgodby in Howdenshire knew Father Atkinson very well and in her Memoirs of 1620 has left a graphic description of his work. 'For several years, he travelled on foot, enduring all weathers, and many times when he had a weary and wet day, the houses to which he went could not receive him in, but that he must stay in some out-house or corner, he being both wet and cold, and in time of frost and snow, to such time as the owners of the houses could for their safety receive him in'.

In his later years, possibly when he was in his sixties, Father Atkinson fell in the snow and broke his leg. A clumsy surgeon set it badly and the priest had to give up his walking and travel by horse.

In 1616 Father Atkinson was visiting the Catholic family of Vavasour at Willitoft, not far from Howden, when his presence was observed and reported. He was arrested, and, despite his age, was tied to a horse and taken to prison in York. He refused to admit his priesthood, lest such admission should incriminate Mr Peter Vavasour and his wife and young children, and firmly rejected the Oath of Allegiance which would have saved his own life. At his trial, the Court experienced great difficulty in proving that he was a priest; although many people knew him to be a priest, none would testify against him. Only when the pursuivants produced the rosary beads and grains of incense they had found on his person was he convicted.

On the scaffold he was shown little mercy and suffered bravely the full rigour of the law in all its cruelty.

74. *John Thules* seminary priest

Born at Whalley, near Blackburn in Lancashire, in 1568
Hanged, drawn and quartered at Lancaster on 18 March, 1616, aged 48

JOHN THULES was only fifteen when, on 28 May 1583, he entered the English College at Rheims. Later he was sent to the Venerable English College in Rome, where his arrival is recorded for 8 May 1590. He was ordained priest in the Lateran Basilica on 28 March 1592, and needed a special dispensation because he was under the canonical age of twenty-four.

One month after his ordination Father Thules returned to England and took his part in the Catholic controversies of the day. At first he supported the appointment of the Archpriest, but later changed his mind and was one of the Appellants who protested to the Pope on 17 November 1600.

Father Thules spent most of his missionary life of twenty-four years in Lancashire, and it was in Lancashire that he was captured. Towards the end of September 1615 he was staying at the house of Roger Wrenno at Chorley, when he was betrayed by one of his cousins, and priest and host were taken to prison in Lancaster Castle.

Shortly before their trial at the Lenten Assizes of 1616, Father Thules and Mr Wrenno managed to escape. They walked all night but lost their sense of direction and moved in a circle, which brought them back to Lancaster at day-break. There they were soon recognised and re-arrested. Father Thules was sentenced to death for his priesthood; and, though offered his life if he would take the Oath of Allegiance, he firmly refused.

During his earlier life, he had had many differences with the Jesuits but from his death cell he sent to each English Jesuit a gift of one angel (a gold coin worth six shillings and eight pence) as a token of his love and esteem. On the scaffold he comported himself with dignity. He prayed for God's mercy and asked the Catholics present to pray for his soul. Before his death he boldly confessed that he was indeed a Catholic priest ordained in Rome.

75. Roger Wrenno Layman

Born at Chorley in Lancashire in 1576
Hanged at Lancaster on 18 March, 1616, aged 60

ROGER WRENNO was a weaver by trade and it was in his house at Chorley that Father John Thules was captured. Mr Wrenno was arrested at the same time and brought to trial at Lancaster Assizes, where he was accused of the felony of harbouring the priest. For this he was sentenced to death and refused to save himself by taking the Oath of Allegiance.

When the time came for his execution, he had first to watch as his friend, Father Thules was hanged, drawn and quartered. Then the rope was put round his own neck and he was suspended. Unfortunately the rope broke and he fell to the ground unconscious but still alive. As they searched for another rope he recovered his senses and was immediately offered his life if he would take the Oath of Allegiance. Once more he refused and resolutely summoned all his strength to climb the ladder for his second hanging.

76. *William Southerne* seminary priest

Born at Ketton, Aycliffe, near Darlington in County Durham in 1579
Hanged, drawn and quartered at Newcastle upon Tyne on 30 April, 1618, aged 39

WILLIAM SOUTHERNE was born to a strongly recusant family and in 1589 his father was in such trouble for his religion that he sent his ten-year-old son out of the country for safety's sake and enrolled him in the Jesuit College at Vilna in Lithuania. Five years later the boy returned home suffering from a chest complaint and spent some time in recuperation before crossing the seas again to continue his education. He was admitted to the English College at Douai in 1596 and seems to have moved backwards and forwards several times between Douai and the English College at Valladolid before he was ordained priest in Spain, probably in 1604.

Father Southerne worked as a priest in the north-eastern counties of England and from Miss A.M.C. Forster's researches (*Recusant History* IV, pp.199-216), it is known that he was in Corbridge, Northumberland in 1606; at Dilston, the home of Sir Francis Radcliffe, in 1608; in Yorkshire in 1610 and in Newcastle upon Tyne in 1615.

In 1618 he was betrayed to Lord Sheffield, the President of the Council of the North, when information was laid against him by William Johnson, a Government spy who had formerly been a student with the priest at Valladolid. At the Assizes in Newcastle upon Tyne on 20 April 1618, Father Southerne was found guilty of his priesthood and sentenced to death. He immediately fell on his knees and thanked God, and when he was offered his life in return for the Oath of Allegiance, he resolutely refused.

The execution of this priest in Newcastle upon Tyne caused repercussions far away in Whitehall. At this time, King James I was at a delicate stage in his negotiations with the King of Spain for the marriage of Prince Charles and the Infanta Maria, and the King had already given his word that the persecution of the Catholics would cease. He tried to assure the King of Spain that he had known nothing about the death of Father Southerne and promised that whoever was responsible would be punished. Lord Sheffield ceased to be President of the Council of the North and no priest was put to death in England for the next ten years.

77. *Thomas Bullaker* Franciscan priest

Born at Midhurst near Chichester in Sussex in 1603
Hanged, drawn and quartered at Tyburn on 12 October, 1642, aged 39

THOMAS BULLAKER was the son of a Catholic doctor of medicine in Chichester. Both his parents were recusants and before he reached the age of eighteen Thomas himself had twice been presented for recusancy. He stayed at the Jesuit College in St Omer for three weeks and was then sent to the English College at Valladolid where his entry is recorded for 29 December 1621. In 1622 he entered the novitiate of the Spanish Franciscans at Abrojo near Valladolid and took the name of John Baptist when he made his profession the following year. After ordination in 1627 or 1628, he contemplated a missionary vocation in the West Indies but was advised that England had a prior claim on his services, and with the approval of the Minister General he set out for the English mission.

Father Bullaker landed at Plymouth in the winter of 1630 but was reported to the authorities by the captain of his ship and immediately arrested. He was interrogated by the Mayor of Plymouth and sent to Exeter for trial. The provisions of the Act of 1585 against the priests were still in force, but the judge hesitated to condemn him to death and he was remanded in custody. The Catholics of Exeter then practised a little forgery to produce a document which secured the release of the priest.

For the next twelve years Father Bullaker worked in the London area. There was at that time a lull in the storm of persecutions as the Queen, Henrietta Maria, the Catholic wife of King Charles I, used her influence to help her co-religionists. Father Bullaker was able to work in peace and used every opportunity to bring Mass and the sacraments to the inhabitants of London. In 1640, however, the Long Parliament complained that the King was being too lenient towards the Catholics and the persecution was renewed in full vigour. On 11 September 1642, Father Bullaker was saying Mass in the house of Mrs Margaret Powell when James Wadsworth, the notorious priest-hunter, burst in and dragged the priest from the altar to prison.

Father Bullaker was interrogated by the Sheriff of London but there seems to have been some doubt as to whether the law should be enforced. The matter was referred first to a special committee of Parliament and then to the Lord Chief Justice before the decision was taken to proceed with the trial.

At the Newgate Sessions on 5 October Father Bullaker was found guilty of his priesthood and sentenced to death as a traitor. He admitted he was a priest but denied that he was a traitor. He refused to compromise his faith by taking the Oath of Allegiance and went willingly to his martyr's death at Tyburn.

78. Henry Heath Franciscan priest

Born at Peterborough, Northamptonshire in 1599
Hanged, drawn and quartered at Tyburn on 17 April, 1643, aged 44

IN 1617 HENRY HEATH was a member of Corpus Christi College, Cambridge. After graduating BA in 1621 he stayed on at the University and took orders in the Church of England on 30 October 1622. He was much influenced in his theology by reading the works of St Robert Bellarmine, and decided to become a Catholic.

He crossed the seas to the English College at Douai, but stayed only a few weeks before finding his true vocation with the English Franciscans in their recently established convent in the city. At his religious profession he took the name of Paul of St Magdalen, and after ordination as a priest began teaching theology to the Franciscan students.

For more than fifteen years he lived this hidden Franciscan life. He practised great austerity and earned a reputation for an extraordinary holiness. At first he had little inclination towards the English Mission, but in 1641 he began to petition his Superiors for permission to work for souls in his own country and in 1643 they granted him his wish.

Father Heath was determined to live to the full the Franciscan ideal of poverty and so set out for England with no money for his journey. He begged his passage to Dover and then walked the seventy miles to London. He sought shelter at the Star Inn near

London Bridge but was soon ejected when the landlord discovered he could not pay. Tired after his long journey, Father Heath rested in the doorway of a house but the householder objected and called on the authorities to remove this unwelcome vagrant. When they arrived, they searched him and discovered a document which stated plainly that he was a priest. He was arrested and taken to prison, interrogated by Isaac Pennington, the Lord Mayor of London, and taken before a special committee of Parliament for further questioning. On each occasion he freely admitted that he was a priest and insisted that he had come to England to save souls.

At the Newgate Sessions on 11 April 1643 he was formally tried and found guilty of his priesthood. When the judge sentenced him to death Father Heath thanked the Court for 'the singular honour' they had shown him, saying 'he was going to die for Christ'.

On Father Heath's final day on earth he wrote and signed a firm rejection of the Oath of Supremacy and was then dragged across London on a hurdle to Tyburn, where he achieved the martyr's death he so much desired.

79. Arthur Bell Franciscan priest

Born at Temple Broughton, Hanbury, Worcestershire on 13 January, 1591
Hanged, drawn and quartered at Tyburn on 11 December, 1643, aged 52

ARTHUR BELL spent one year at the Jesuit school of St Omer and then, in September 1615, went on to the English College at Valladolid. He was ordained priest at Salamanca on 14 April 1618. He entered the Franciscan novitiate at Segovia and was solemnly professed on 8 September 1619, taking Francis as his name in religion. In October 1620 he left the Spanish Franciscans and moved to Douai to assist Father John Gennings in re-establishing the English Province of the Order. He took part in the first Chapter of the restored Province in December 1630 and was appointed Guardian of the Douai house, where he continued his studying, lecturing and writing. In 1633 he was entrusted with the foundation of a Scottish Province, but when these plans failed he came to the English mission and worked in the London area for the next nine years.

Father Bell was arrested on 6 November 1643. He was travelling on horse-back from Brigstock in Northamptonshire to London when he was stopped at a check-point set up by Parliamentary soldiers at Stevenage in Hertfordshire. At first he was suspected of being a royalist spy but when he was searched three papers were discovered which aroused the suspicion that he was a priest (Stone, *Faithful unto Death*, p.184). He was interrogated by the authorities in Hertford and then by a Parliamentary Committee in London. As a result of these examinations, he was committed to prison in Newgate as 'a Franciscan confessed and a Roman priest suspected'.

As the trial of Father Bell opened at the Newgate Sessions on Thursday 7 December 1643 there was a great outbreak of anti-Catholic feeling in the city, for it was the very day on which a Parliamentary paper was published to inform all England that secret letters from the Archbishop of Cambrai had been intercepted and that Pope Urban VIII had set up the Ordinary Process for the beatification of those English Catholics who had died for their Faith. The hostility aroused by this news prevented all further progress in the Cause of the English Martyrs for over two hundred years and, as one of the letters discovered was addressed to Father Bell, he became a primary object of the anger aroused. Bishop Challoner is certain that this hastened his execution.

The French Ambassador, the Comte d'Harcourt, endeavoured to secure the priest's release, but all his efforts were in vain. On 11 December Father Bell said Mass in his cell at Newgate and was taken to Tyburn to die as a Catholic priest no longer suspected but now admitted.

80. *Edward Bamber* seminary priest

Born at Carlton, Poulton-le-Fylde, Lancashire about 1600
Hanged, drawn and quartered at Lancaster on 7 August, 1646, aged about 46

WHEN EDWARD BAMBER was about sixteen years of age he left the Catholic surrounds of his home in the Fylde and journeyed across England to Newcastle upon Tyne, from which port he sailed to Flanders and the Jesuit College of St Omer. Two and a half years later he made another dangerous sea voyage from Calais to Sanlucar de Barrameda in southern Spain and then proceeded to Seville, where he entered the English College in 1621. On 6 June 1626 he was ordained priest at Cadiz.

Father Bamber took to the sea again for his return journey to England, but his French ship sprang a leak in the English Channel and put into Plymouth for repairs. Here the priest was arrested, questioned and committed to prison. He was not able to stand up to the pressure and conformed to the State Church at least in an exterior manner. The Archbishop of Canterbury issued him with a Royal Pardon and he was set free.

For the next sixteen years Father Bamber worked as a priest in Lancashire, and the excellence of his apostolate suggests that he made full amends for whatever weakness he may have shown in Plymouth. Father John Knaresborough (1720) writes about 'his unwearied diligence in instructing the Catholics committed to his charge, disputing with Protestants, and going about to do good everywhere, in times and places of the greatest danger, with a courage and firmness of mind much spoken of and admired at that time'.

Father Bamber was arrested again sometime in 1643 but, with the Civil War raging, the judges were unable to conduct their business and the priest was kept in Lancaster Castle for the next three years. With him in prison were two other priests, Father John Woodcock and Father Thomas Whittaker, and all three were brought to trial at the same time when the judges returned in August 1646.

Two former Catholics gave evidence against Father Bamber that they had seen him administer baptism and perform the ceremonies of marriage; and on the strength of these statements, the judge ordered the jury to bring in a verdict of guilty. Father Bamber was the first of the three priests to die and was actually encouraging his companions in their determination when the Sheriff hastily ordered the hangman to turn him off the ladder.

81. *John Woodcock* Franciscan priest

Born at Clayton-le-Woods, Leyland, Lancashire in 1603
Hanged, drawn and quartered at Lancaster on 7 August, 1646, aged 43

JOHN WOODCOCK became a Catholic when he was about twenty years of age and this action so angered his Protestant father that the young man had to leave home and stay with his mother's family, the Catholic Andertons. In 1628 he crossed to the Continent to the Jesuit College at St Omer, and on 20 October 1629 he became a student in Rome at the Venerable English College.

Within six months of his arrival in Rome John Woodcock reached the conviction that he had a Franciscan vocation and he set out for the Capuchin novitiate in Paris. Through no fault of his own he survived only a few months and was then dismissed. After some hesitation he offered himself to the English Friars Minor in Douai where he was accepted and professed as Martin of St Felix in 1632. In 1634 he was ordained priest.

For the next nine years, Father Woodcock worked as a priest in Flanders. At first he was chaplain to an English gentleman, Mr Sheldon, at Arras, and then chaplain to the English Franciscan nuns at Nieuport. At this point his health broke down and he had to return to the Franciscan house at Douai. On Trinity Sunday, 1643, Father Woodcock attended the solemn service of thanksgiving for the martyrdom of Father Henry Heath and was so moved by the example of this holy Franciscan from whom he had received the Franciscan habit that he begged his Superiors to send him to England.

Father Woodcock landed at Newcastle upon Tyne and from there returned to Lancashire to visit his family. His protestant father was too frightened to receive him and there is evidence to support the local tradition that all he did was give his son breakfast and send him away. The priest was captured a short distance from his home and sent to Lancaster Castle, where he remained for three years with Father Edward Bamber and Father Thomas Whittaker until the Assizes were re-commenced after the initial upsets of the Civil War.

At his trial Father Woodcock admitted that he was a priest and a Franciscan friar, and on this evidence was condemned to death. He was the second of the three priests to die at Lancaster on 7 August 1646.

82. Thomas Whittaker seminary priest

Born in Burnley, Lancashire in 1611
Hanged, drawn and quartered at Lancaster on 7 August, 1646, aged 35

THOMAS WHITTAKER was the son of a Catholic schoolmaster and was only eleven years of age when he was sent across the seas to the Jesuit school at St Omer. Twelve years later, in 1634, he was admitted to the English College at Valladolid and was ordained priest there in 1638. Coming to the English mission he worked for five years in his native Lancashire and a List of Clergy for 1639 names him as being in Goosnargh in the north of the county.

From Father John Knaresborough's evidence it would seem that Father Whittaker was arrested at Blake Hall, the home of the Midgall family, in the parish of Goosnargh on about 7 August 1643. His captors lacked evidence that he was a priest and beat him with clubs until he confessed.

With Father Edward Bamber and Father John Woodcock, Father Whittaker had to wait three years in Lancaster Castle for the arrival of the judges. At first he was kept in solitary confinement but later mixed with his fellow prisoners. Father Knaresborough says that he was 'a person by nature very timorous even to a fault' but he knew this himself and as the time for his trial approached he prepared himself by a month's retreat of prayer and fasting for the courage to undergo his ordeal.

Everybody seems to have been aware of Father Whittaker's struggle within himself. On the scaffold his two companions exhorted him to fortitude, but as he watched them die in agony he seems to have lost heart, at least for a moment, and his captors pressed their advantage by repeating their offers of freedom if he would deny his Faith. Then suddenly they lost patience with him and brusquely told him to make up his mind at once 'Summoning up his spirits', as Father Knaresborough has said, 'he boldly told the Sheriff his resolution was fixed to die in the profession of the Catholic Faith. Use your pleasure with me', he said; 'a reprieve or even a pardon, upon your conditions, I utterly refuse'. With these words he followed Father Bamber and Father Woodcock to martyrdom.

83. Nicholas Postgate seminary priest

Born at Kirkdale House, Egton Bridge, North Yorkshire in 1599
Hanged, drawn and quartered at York on 7 August, 1679, aged 80

NICHOLAS POSTGATE was twenty-two years of age when he entered the English College at Douai on 4 July 1621. He was ordained priest at Arras on 20 March 1628. On coming to the English mission he first stayed with the Hungate family at Saxton near Tadcaster in West Yorkshire, but in 1642 he moved to the East Riding, to Burton Constable and then Halsham, where he was chaplain to Lady Dunbar until her death in 1659. Later he was chaplain to another branch of the Constable family at Everingham, and a strong tradition affirms that he served the Meynell family at Kilvington Castle and the Saltmarshe family at Kilvington Hall in the North Riding.

Father Postgate moved away from the country houses of the wealthy Catholics and in the early 1660s became a travelling priest for his own poor people on the North Yorkshire Moors. He lived in poverty in an isolated thatched cottage called the Hermitage near Ugthorpe, and despite being more than sixty years of age he actively covered an extensive territory from Guisborough to Pickering for almost twenty years.

The anti-Catholic agitation which followed the fictitious plot of Titus Oates was responsible for Father Postgate's capture. The priest was baptising a baby on 8 December 1678, at Littlebeck near Whitby, when an exciseman, John Reeves, burst in and arrested him. A search of the house revealed relics, altar breads and Catholic books which the priest admitted were his. He was taken to Brompton for interrogation and then to prison in York Castle.

At the Lenten Assizes in York in March 1679 Father Postgate was found guilty of his priesthood and sentenced to death. He was kept in York Castle for another four months while the Government debated the advisibility of continuing the policy of executing priests but on 11 July, the Privy Council decided that Father Postgate should die. The venerable old priest was happy to accept his fate but made it very clear in his last speech from the scaffold that he was dying 'not for the Plot but for my religion'.

Father Postgate has been remembered in a remarkable way by the people of Yorkshire and his memory is still fresh among his own people in the moorland parishes of Egton Bridge and Ugthorpe.

84. Charles Meehan Franciscan priest

Born in Ireland about 1640
Hanged, drawn and quartered at Ruthin, Denbighshire on 12 August, 1679, aged about 39

FATHER CHARLES MEEHAN arrived in England by chance. He was on his way from Rome to Ireland when he was shipwrecked off the English Coast, and was merely travelling through North Wales towards one of the ports for Ireland when he was arrested on the suspicion that he was a Catholic priest.

Father Meehan was a Franciscan. He had been ordained priest before 1672 when he was approved as a confessor in Rome. In 1674 he was at the Irish Franciscan College in Louvain, and he spent some time at the Franciscan house at Hammellburg in Germany before returning to Rome to St Isidore's College, in 1676.

By June 1678 Father Meehan was in custody in Denbigh, but there were legal delays. The vital evidence of the Catholic books and papers found on his person was sent to London and not returned until September and there was much correspondence between Sir John Salusbury, the local Justice of the Peace, and Sir Joseph Williamson, the Secretary of State in London, as to whether the case should proceed or not. It was not until 29 September that the decision was made to bring the priest to trial.

It was Father Meehan's misfortune that this was the time when the anti-Catholic agitation associated with the alleged Plot revealed by Titus Oates swept the country, and it was at its height when he was brought to trial at the Great Sessions for Denbighshire on 28 April 1679.

He was charged not with any involvement in the Plot but simply with being a priest. This he readily admitted; but the facts that he was just passing through England, that he had not exercised his ministry and that he had no intention to exercise it in England, were not allowed to influence the judgement of the court. He was found guilty and sentenced to death.

In his final address from the scaffold Father Meehan said he was suffering for his religion, and he forgave those who had brought about his death and prayed for them as well as for those who had helped him. He asked God to bless the King and convert him to the Catholic Faith.

85. George Douglas priest

Born in Edinburgh; date unknown
Hanged, drawn and quartered at York on 9 September, 1587

GEORGE DOUGLAS was a Scotsman, and his Cause has been included among the Causes of the English and Welsh Martyrs at the request of the Scottish Bishops. Unfortunately it would seem that there were three priests called George Douglas working in England at that time, and the details of the earlier life of the George Douglas, undoubtedly martyred at York in 1587, are difficult to decipher.

It has been established that as a youth George Douglas escaped from Scotland to the Continent and then came to England where he worked as a schoolmaster in Rutland from about 1568. He went abroad again in 1574 and was ordained priest in the cathedral of Notre Dame in Paris, but for the next ten years his whereabouts are not known.

About July 1584 Father Douglas began a journey home to Scotland. He was robbed by pirates on the voyage from Flushing to Calais and although he was granted a travel permit through England by the Mayor of Dover, this was stolen from him in Gravesend. He was obliged to travel north without proper papers and was accordingly arrested at Glaston in Rutland. He was kept in custody for a short time and then released.

Perhaps he was still making his slow way north to the Scottish border when he was arrested again in Ripon in the West Riding of Yorkshire. He was accused of speaking out against married priests and was kept in a dark dungeon for a year. From Ripon he was taken to York to join the other Catholic prisoners in York Castle, and here he was kept for another year.

Father Douglas was brought to trial at the Lenten Sessions in York in 1587. It was not possible for him to be charged under the Statute of 1585 because this applied to Englishmen ordained priests overseas. It is more likely that he was charged with 'persuading to popery' which was also a capital offence. Whatever the charge, he was condemned to death for his religion and the Catholics of his time had no doubt at all that he was executed because he was a priest, for his name is included in all the principal Catalogues of Martyrs from 1590 onwards.

Index